美剧与美国社会文化

主　编　王琳梅　秦晓星
副主编　管云秋　苑晓鹤

图书在版编目(CIP)数据

美剧与美国社会文化/王琳梅,秦晓星主编. —北京:北京大学出版社,2013.2
(大学英语立体化网络化系列教材·拓展课程教材)

ISBN 978-7-301-22008-5

Ⅰ.①美… Ⅱ.①王…②秦… Ⅲ.①英语-听说教学-高等学校-教材 Ⅳ.① H319.9

中国版本图书馆CIP数据核字(2013)第016438号

书　　　名:	美剧与美国社会文化
著作责任者:	王琳梅　秦晓星　主编
责任编辑:	黄瑞明
标准书号:	ISBN 978-7-301-22008-5/H·3238
出版发行:	北京大学出版社
地　　　址:	北京市海淀区成府路205号　100871
网　　　址:	http://www.pup.cn　新浪官方微博:@北京大学出版社
电子信箱:	zbing@pup.pku.edu.cn
电　　　话:	邮购部 62752015　发行部 62750672　编辑部 62754382　出版部 62754962
印　刷　者:	北京虎彩文化传播有限公司
经　销　者:	新华书店

　　　　　　787毫米×1092毫米　16开本　10.5印张　200千字
　　　　　　2013年2月第1版　2022年5月第5次印刷

定　　　价:39.00元

未经许可,不得以任何方式复制或抄袭本书之部分或全部内容。
版权所有,侵权必究　　举报电话:010-62752024
　　　　　　　　　　　电子信箱:fd@pup.pku.edu.cn

Preface

　　教育部高等教育司发布的《大学英语课程教学要求》中提到,"大学英语课程不仅是一门语言基础课程,也是拓宽知识、了解世界文化的素质教育课程,兼有工具性和人文性。因此,设计大学英语课程时也应当充分考虑对学生的文化素质培养和国际文化知识的传授。"

　　近些年,看美剧不仅在高校学生中成为一种新时尚,而且也成为继《新概念》、《走遍美国》、英美电影、VOA 及 BBC 新闻英语后,高校学生学习英语的一种新方式。美剧的确是学习英语的一种很好的材料。从增加语言知识和提高语言技能的角度上说,看美剧可以增加词汇量,提高听力技能;从了解目的语国家文化的角度看,美剧题材广泛、贴近生活、对话量大,并且对话充斥着习惯用法和美国人独有的思维方式,因此看美剧能帮助学生了解目的语国家的生活、文化、风俗和思维方式,学到真正能用来交际的英语。不仅如此,通过看美剧学习语言,形式生动、活泼,不会枯燥无趣,有助于保持并提高学生学习语言的兴趣。

　　但是,在海量的美剧面前,如何选择并有效利用以促进英语的学习,对许多人而言,是很茫然的事情。因此,编写组四位老师结合大学英语学习目标和大学生的兴趣,针对一些热点社会问题,考虑语言及反映的社会、文化问题等两方面,从近些年受关注及获奖的美剧中挑选了适合作为语言学习材料的 13 部美剧作为素材,共观看了约七百集,从中剪辑并精心挑选了 12 个视频,作为教材编写的视频素材。在此基础上,又从语言学习及文化素养培养的角度精心设计、编写了本教材,内容丰富、实用。

　　本教程有以下特点:

　　1. 培养综合技能: 本教材不仅旨在全面提高学生基本语言技能,还引导学生从社会学的角度剖析、比较并了解中美两国社会特点及文化背景等,拓宽知识面,更深入地了解目的语国家社会及文化,并进一步加深对祖国文化的理解,为成为国际型人才打好基础。就语言技能而言,听、说、读、写、译五项技能全部覆盖;就社会文化而言,以英国社会学家 Anthony Giddens 的 *Sociology* 目录为基础,覆盖了美国社会的 12 个主要方面。

　　2. 语言材料地道真实: 中国学生学习英语的语言环境匮乏,如何创造地道真实的语境一直是学者和一线教师努力的目标。本教材视频材料取材于反映美国文化生活的美国电视剧,保证了语言的地道性、真实性。

　　3. 选材丰富、有趣味: 本教材从学生的兴趣和需要出发编写。编者选择的视频材料功能、风格丰富,有正式场合如总统的就职演说,有日常生活的家长里短,有紧张的恐怖袭击,

美剧与美国社会文化

有搞笑的人际交往片段等等。

本教材结构及单元每部分要求:

本教材共12单元,每单元包括六部分:

1) Part Ⅰ: Story Exploration

本部分以泛听为主,熟悉视频主要内容(人物关系、主要故事情节等)。

2) Part Ⅱ: Language Appreciation

本部分以精听为主,学习地道美语表达。在语言输入的基础上,通过配音、表演等模仿活动,提高并完善语音、语调等发音技能。

3) Words and Expressions

为方便学生学习,本部分罗列了本单元视频出现的生词及专有名称,并配有音标及例句。

4) Part Ⅲ: Culture and Society Focus

就本单元视频反映的社会问题,本部分提供了相关资料,学生首先进行阅读,了解相关信息并熟悉相关表达;接下来通过有关该话题的口语活动,深入探讨此社会问题,并口头表达出自己的想法。

5) Part Ⅳ: Writing

本部分要求学生围绕口语活动探讨的话题,进行写作练习。

依据作文的成文顺序,编者在各章分别给出 Functional Sentence Patterns,比如如何写议论文的开头、主体和结尾等,引导学生以清晰的思路、丰富的表达进行写作。

6) Additional Information

本部分提供与该美剧或演员相关的信息,提高学生学习兴趣。

本教材由四位中国海洋大学从事大学英语教学一线工作多年的老师通力合作编写而成。其中王琳梅负责编写第二、九及十一单元,秦晓星负责编写第七、八、十二单元,管云秋负责编写第一、四、五单元,苑晓鹤负责编写第六、十单元,第三单元由王琳梅、秦晓星共同编写。

本教材的编写工作得到了中国海洋大学外国语学院英语二系王慧敏主任的大力支持和鼓励。除此之外,在素材搜集、视频编辑及课件制作等方面,还得到很多人的支持和帮助:中国海洋大学2009级港口航道海岸工程专业本科生于丹同学为编写组提供了20部(约150G)美剧视频;潘梦寒先生、张兴斌先生、王英杰先生和王向进先生为编写组提供了技术上的支持。

在他们的帮助下,编写组得以高效、顺利地完成编写工作,在此致以诚挚的感谢。

鉴于各种原因,书中难免有纰漏,望使用者和老师们不吝赐教!

编者
2012年7月

CONTENTS

	Preface	
	Immigration	
	Part I Story Exploration	1
Unit 1	Part II Language Appreciation	2
	Part III Culture and Society Focus	5
	Part IV Writing	10
	Additional Information	11
	Depression	
	Part I Story Exploration	12
Unit 2	Part II Language Appreciation	15
	Part III Culture and Society Focus	18
	Part IV Writing	23
	Additional Information	23
	Aging	
	Part I Story Exploration	25
Unit 3	Part II Language Appreciation	26
	Part III Culture and Society Focus	29
	Part IV Writing	34
	Additional Information	35

Unit 4	**Gender and Love**	
	Part Ⅰ Story Exploration	37
	Part Ⅱ Language Appreciation	39
	Part Ⅲ Culture and Society Focus	42
	Part Ⅳ Writing	46
	Additional Information	47
Unit 5	**Nonmarital Pregnancy**	
	Part Ⅰ Story Exploration	49
	Part Ⅱ Language Appreciation	51
	Part Ⅲ Culture and Society Focus	54
	Part Ⅳ Writing	60
	Additional Information	61
Unit 6	**Voting and Elections**	
	Part Ⅰ Story Exploration	63
	Part Ⅱ Language Appreciation	64
	Part Ⅲ Culture and Society Focus	68
	Part Ⅳ Writing	74
	Additional Information	74
Unit 7	**Terrorism and Prejudices**	
	Part Ⅰ Story Exploration	77
	Part Ⅱ Language Appreciation	79
	Part Ⅲ Culture and Society Focus	82
	Part Ⅳ Writing	87
	Additional Information	87

CONTENTS

Unit 8	**Gender and Work**	
	Part I Story Exploration	89
	Part II Language Appreciation	91
	Part III Culture and Society Focus	94
	Part IV Writing	98
Unit 9	**Gun Violence**	
	Part I Story Exploration	101
	Part II Language Appreciation	103
	Part III Culture and Society Focus	105
	Part IV Writing	113
	Additional Information	113
Unit 10	**Crime Correction**	
	Part I Story Exploration	115
	Part II Language Appreciation	118
	Part III Culture and Society Focus	122
	Part IV Writing	128
	Additional Information	129
Unit 11	**Poverty**	
	Part I Story Exploration	130
	Part II Language Appreciation	132
	Part III Culture and Society Focus	135
	Part IV Writing	141
	Additional Information	142

Unit 12	**Education and Inequality**	
	Part Ⅰ　　Story Exploration	143
	Part Ⅱ　　Language Appreciation	145
	Part Ⅲ　　Culture and Society Focus	148
	Part Ⅳ　　Writing	153
	Additional Information	154
Appendix I	Useful Expressions in a Discussion/ Debate	156
Appendix II	Emmy Award	158

Unit 1

Immigration

> In this unit, you will:
> - watch video clips from *Ugly Betty*;
> - understand the lines from it;
> - learn something about *immigration*;
> - learn some expressions on *introducing a topic (I)*.

Part I Story Exploration

Section A Character Introduction

Background:

Mode: *a trendy, high fashion magazine that is part of the publishing empire of the wealthy Bradford Meade.*

Bradford: *father of Daniel Meade. Bradford and Wilhelmina are getting married.*

Daniel: *Betty's boss, Editor-in-Chief of Mode magazine.*

Dwayne: *Wilhelmina's bodyguard.*

Hilda: *Betty's sister, who makes a living by selling weight-loss products of Herbalux.*

Characters that will appear in this video clip:

Wilhelmina **Betty** **Hilda** **Ignacio**

Watch the video clip, and tell what you know about Ignacio.

Betty's father,

Section B Story Retelling

Watch the video clip again, then work in pairs and retell the story with the help of the following questions.

1. What does the social worker tell about Betty's father?

2. According to the lawyer, how serious is the problem? What are they supposed to do about it?

3. What are Betty and her sister doing at home? What irritates the father?

4. Why does Betty's father never apply for a green card or begin a citizenship process?

5. Why does Hilda say they have to make some serious cutbacks?

6. What is the deal between Wilhelmina and Betty?

7. What is the end of the story?

Part II Language Appreciation

Section A Language Input

Task 1 Watch the video clip twice and fill in the missing information (one blank for one word).

Woman: I'm sorry, but your father's not _____ _____ _____ _____ _____.
Betty: I don't know what you're talking about.
Woman: According to our _____, Ignacio Suarez is 117 years old... and dead.
Betty: Well, obviously that's a mistake.
Woman: Not on our end. The _____ _____ _____ your father's been using belongs to somebody else.

Unit 1 Immigration

Hilda: Betty... We have to make some serious _____. The pharmacy wouldn't fill his _____ today.

Betty: What? Maria Ortiz...she can't do that. She knows he needs his _____ to work. He has arrhythmia. He could die.

Hilda: It wasn't Maria. It's his H.M.O. They're not gonna _____ _____ _____.

All: I hereby _____ _____ _____ that I absolutely and entirely renounce and abjure all allegiance and fidelity to any foreign _____, state or sovereignty, of whom or which I have heretofore been a _____ or citizen.

Justin: Gwyneth's wearing white to the wedding? That is such a bitch slap.

All: That I will support and defend the _____ and _____ of the United States of America against all enemies, enemy: foreign and domestic, that I will _____ and allegiance to the same.

Task 2 Watch the video clip, and get the English expressions for the following Chinese phrases or sentences.

出生证明	
使经历……	
勒紧裤腰带	
充分运用时间	
减肥	
撕掉	
初恋	
支持	
脱身,逃脱	

Task 3 Translate the following lines into English, pay special attention to the parts in color, and then watch the video clip and check.

1. Betty: 他可能会被遣返?
   Man: 是的,很有可能。

   _____

   _____

2. 鉴于你们提供的信息来看,你们的父亲正处于紧要关头。

   _____

3. 政府正在调查,而最后,法官可能会判定将你遣返墨西哥。

   _____

4. 那时我正忙着养家糊口。
_____.

Section B Language Output

Watch video clips in this section, and then choose one clip to dub or role play.
Clip 1: Betty—Hilda—Ignacio—lawyer
Clip 2: Betty—Hilda—Ignacio
Clip 3: Betty—Wilhelmina

Words and Expressions

Words

deport	[dɪˈpɔːt]	vt.	驱逐出境；持……举止
ultimately	[ˈʌltɪmɪtli]	adv.	最后，最终
amnesty	[ˈæmnesti]	n.	大赦，特赦
probono			【拉】为慈善机构和穷人提供的免费专业服务
fiber	[ˈfaɪbə]	n.	纤维（物质）
retainer	[rɪˈteɪnə]	n.	（律师、顾问等的）聘金
grand	[grænd]	n.	一千美元
validate	[ˈvælɪdeɪt]	vt.	使生效；证实，确认，验证
certificate	[səˈtɪfɪkɪt]	n.	执照，证（明）书
passport	[ˈpɑːspɔːt]	n.	护照
naked	[ˈneɪkɪd]	adj.	裸体的
document	[ˈdɔkjumənt]	n.	文件，公文，文档
tease	[tiːz]	v.	戏弄
hook	[huk]	n.	钩，钩状物；勾拳
heel	[hiːl]	n.	脚后跟
chef	[ʃef]	n.	厨师
vow	[vau]	v.	发誓
prescription	[prɪsˈkrɪpʃn]	n.	处方，药方；对策
visa	[ˈviːzə]	n.	签证
loyalty	[ˈlɔɪəlti]	n.	忠诚
oath	[əuθ]	n.	誓言，誓约
renounce	[rɪˈnauns]	v.	声明放弃，与……断绝关系
abjure	[əbˈdʒuə]	v.	发誓弃绝，公开放弃

Unit 1　Immigration

allegiance	[əˈliːdʒəns]	n.	忠诚,效忠
fidelity	[fiˈdeləti]	n.	忠实,忠诚
sovereignty	[ˈsɔvrənti]	n.	主权,独立国
slap	[slæp]	n.	侮辱;掴;拍击声
constitution	[ˌkɔnstiˈtjuːʃən]	n.	宪法;组织;体质
domestic	[dəˈmestik]	adj.	家庭的;国内的;驯养的

Phrases and Idioms

tighten one's belt: to spend less than one did before because one has less money 勒紧裤腰带
— I've had to tighten my belt since I stopped working full-time.

set up: to establish in business by providing capital, equipment, or other backing; to prepare 资助;为……做准备
— His father's money left Jim well set up for life.

off the hook: to be proven not guilty of something; to escape one's responsibility or duty 逃脱,脱身
— You think god will let you off the hook?

hold all the cards: to have all the advantages in a situation in which people are competing or arguing 处于非常强势(或有利)的位置
— "There's not much we can do. They seem to hold all the cards," said Dan gloomily.

Proper Names

Herbalux: a health supplement company 保健品公司
H.M.O.: short for health maintenance organization 医保机构

Part III　Culture and Society Focus

Immigration in the U.S.	
	Immigration Terms
	US Immigration Facts and Statistics
	Illegal Immigration Facts and Statistics
	Reasons of Immigration
	Pros and Cons of Immigration

In this video clip, Ignacio is an illegal immigrant. According to this clip:

- Why did he immigrate illegally?
- What might happen to an illegal immigrant?

Immigration Terms

Immigration (derived from Latin: migratio) is the act of foreigners passing or coming into a country for the purpose of permanent residence. Familiarize with the following terms: "immigrant," "illegal immigrant" and "undocumented immigrant."

- Immigrant—a person who leaves one country to settle permanently in another after being granted permission to do so by the government.
- Illegal immigrant—an alien (non-citizen) who has entered the United States without government permission or stayed beyond the termination date of a visa. This person is sometimes referred to as an *undocumented immigrant*.

US Immigration Facts and Statistics

Immigration has played an important role in shaping the United States of America. It is estimated that an average of 104,000 foreigners arrive each day in the United States. About 2,000 unauthorized foreigners a day settle in the United States. Between 1990 and 2010, the number of foreign-born US residents almost doubled from 20 million to 40 million, while the US population rose from almost 250 million to 310 million.

The leading countries of origin of immigrants to the United States were Mexico, India, the Philippines, and China, as is shown in the following table.

Rank	Country	2010	Percentage
1	Mexico	9,600,000	23.70
2	China	1,900,000	4.70
3	Philippines	1,700,000	4.20
4	India	1,610,000	4.00
5	Vietnam	1,200,000	3.00

Illegal Immigration Facts and Statistics

Each year millions of people cross the U.S. borders illegally in search of the American dream—a land of freedom and opportunity. According to a study by the Pew Hispanic Center based on government figures, the number of illegal immigrants living and working in the country lies somewhere between 11—12 million (2008)(Figure 1), or around one in every 20 workers. Other estimates range from 7 to 20 million.

Unit 1 Immigration

Figure 1

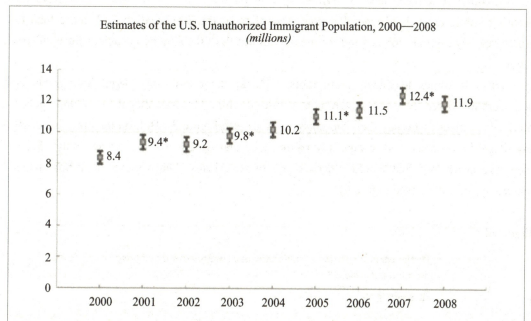

Note: Estimates are based on residual methodology. Bars indicate low and high points of the estimated 90% confidence interval. The symbol * indicates that the change from previous year is statistically significant.

Source: Pew Hispanic Center estimates, 2008, based on March Supplements to the Current Population Survey (CPS).

Reasons of Immigration

Immigrants come to America for many reasons. Family reunification accounts for approximately two-thirds of permanent immigration to the United States each year. Other possible factors include:

- Seeking employment or improved financial position,
- Searching for better educational resources,
- Seeking freedom (Escaping from dictatorship, religious persecution, frequent abuse, oppression, ethnic cleansing and even genocide, and risks to civilians during war),
- Evasion of criminal justice (e.g. avoiding arrest),
- Dramatic decrease in travel time and costs between the 18th and early 20th century,
- Transnational marriage,
- Lack of immigration law enforcement,
- Illegal immigration amnesty and birth right citizenship.

Pros and Cons of Immigration

Although Americans have a divided opinion on the issue of migration, they have been favoring immigration as a general matter. According to the 2008 Gallup Poll, more than half Americans say immigration is good for the overall health of the American society since 2001(see Figure 2).

When it comes to illegal immigrants, 63% of the public say illegal immigrants cost taxpayers too much by using government services, while 31% say illegal immigrants become productive citizens who pay their fair share of taxes (see Figure 3). But, on the other hand, 79% say illegal immigrants tend to take low-paying jobs that Americans don't want, only 15% say they take away jobs that would otherwise go to Americans. These views have not changed materially since 2006 (see Figure 4).

Figure 2

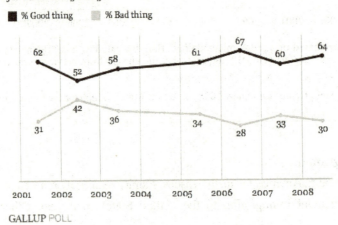

Figure 3

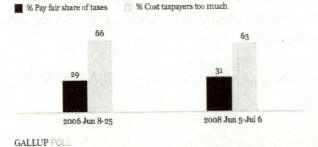

Unit 1　Immigration

Figure 4

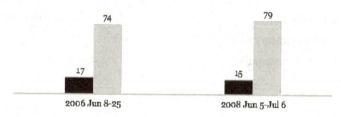

Which comes closer to your view — [ROTATED: illegal immigrants mostly take jobs that American workers want, (or) illegal immigrants mostly take low-paying jobs Americans don't want?]

■ % Take jobs American workers want
▨ % Take low-paying jobs Americans don't want

GALLUP POLL

Task 1　Complete the following table about the advantages and disadvantages of living in the US.

ADVANTAGES	DISADVANTAGES

Task 2　Pair work—create a dialogue on the following situation.

Step 1　Compare your answers in Task 1 with your partner. What ideas do you have in common, and what ideas are different? You can discuss and debate about your points. Try to provide reasons and supporting details.

Step 2　Prepare

Make an outline.

> Topic: **immigrating to America**
> Roles: **Michael and Daniel**
> Situation: **Michael and Daniel are good friends. Michael tells Daniel his idea of immigrating to America and Daniel tries to persuade him not to.**

Dialogue

Michael:

Daniel:

Useful Expressions

living and working environment
child-bearing (policy & hospital)
education
welfare
family, friend
language
sense of belonging
religion
way of thinking
racial bias
uncertainties

Your Own Word Box

Step 3   Rehearse

Practise your dialogue with your partner.

Step 4   Present

Present your dialogue to the class.

Listener task: Take notes of the main points, which might be useful for your writing.

Part IV   Writing

Write about the following topic:

If you had the chance of immigrating to the US, would you accept it? Why or why not? Give reasons for your answer and include any relevant examples.

Write at least 200 words.

Unit 1   Immigration

Functional Sentence Patterns

Introducing a Topic (I)
● Nowadays more and more people are migrating to some developed countries...
● Nowadays there is a growing concern over...
● There are numerous reasons why...
● As to whether it is a blessing or a curse, however, people take different attitudes.
● It cannot be denied that...

Additional Information

Two main characters in *Ugly Betty*	
 Ignacio Suarez portrayed by Tony Plana	**Awards** Satellite Awards for Best Actor in a Supporting Role in a Series, Miniseries, or Motion Picture Made for Television for his role as "Ignacio Suarez," *Ugly Betty*, on December 17, 2006. **Nominations** Screen Actors Guild Awards: Screen Actors Guild Award for Best Ensemble—Comedy Series for: *Ugly Betty* (2006). ALMA Awards: Outstanding Actor in a Television Series for: *Resurrection Blvd* (2002). ALMA Awards: Outstanding Actor in a New Television Series for: *Resurrection Blvd* (2001). Bravo Awards: Outstanding Actor in a Feature Film for: *Lone Star* (1996).
 Betty Suarez portrayed by America Georgina Ferrera	◆ America Georgina Ferrera is an American actress and producer. She is best known for her leading role as "Betty Suarez" on the ABC television series *Ugly Betty* (2006—2010). ◆ She won the Golden Globe Award for Best Actress—Television Series Musical or Comedy, the Screen Actors Guild Award for Outstanding Performance by a Female Actor in a Comedy Series, and the Primetime Emmy Award for Outstanding Leading Actress in a Comedy Series. ◆ She transitioned to a film career, starring in several films aimed at young audiences, including *Real Women Have Curves*, *The Sisterhood of the Traveling Pants*.

Unit 2

Depression

> In this unit, you will:
> - watch video clips from *Lie to Me*;
> - understand the lines from it;
> - know something about *depression*;
> - learn some expressions on *introducing a topic (II)*.

Part I   Story Exploration

Before you watch the video, write down the expression on the face below each picture.
Basically, human beings have 7 micro expressions, they are *sadness, anger, happiness, contempt, surprise, disgust* and *fear*.

  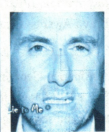 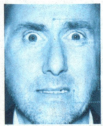

_____   _____   _____   _____

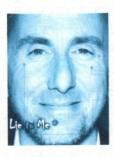 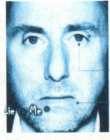 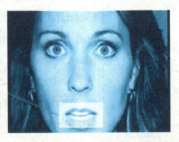

_____   _____   _____

Unit 2 Depression

Section A Character Introduction

Video Clip 1:

Background: *Dr. Lightman is giving a lecture about expressions.*

Watch the video clip, and tell what you can learn from his lecture.

_____.

Video Clip 2:

The names of the characters in this video clip are given in the following table. Watch the video, and match the characters with the identities.

Character Name	Identity
Dr. Foster	pilot, commander
David Markov	assistant of Dr. Foster

13

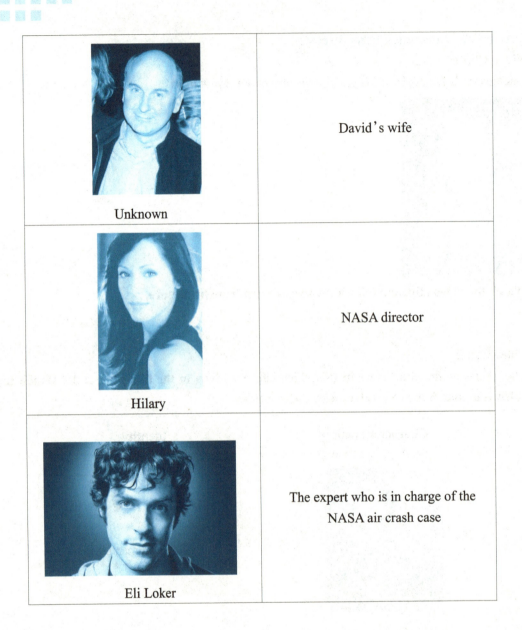

Section B Story Retelling

Watch video clip 2 again, then work in pairs and retell the story with the help of the following questions and words.

Questions	Tip Words
1. What does NASA ask Dr. Foster to do?	NASA, X-48, test flights, crash, investigate
2. What happened according to the pilot?	David Markov, lose track of time, deny, intentionally

3. What does Dr. Foster think of what the pilot tells her?	telling the truth, psychological state prior to the crash, record
4. When Dr. Foster checks the videotapes of the pilot a month ago and 2 weeks ago, does she find any changes? If yes, what are they?	depressed, relaxed
5. What does Hilary tell about the pilot? And what does Dr. Foster learn from this talk?	pressure, competition for the X-48 pilot, handle, drug test
6. What have Dr. Foster and Loker found out?	Tox result, treating depression, self-medicating, side effects
7. What does it turn out to be the cause of the crash?	scared, slip into, dose

Part II Language Appreciation

Section A Language Input

Task 1 Translate the following phrases into English, and then watch the video clip and check.

极速飞行	
能见度很高	
失去时间感	
故意	
非正面回答问题	
400分之一的机会	

Task 2 Watch the video clip twice and fill in the missing words.

Foster: So, captain Markov admitted a _____ of _____ about certain details. He also used spontaneous _____: 10,500 instead of 10,000 feet.

NASA official: So, he's lying?

Loker: No, those are all _____ of telling the truth.

NASA official: Well, our doctors examined him after the crash. Medically, he _____ fine.

Foster: There's another possibility. It's called a hysterical blackout. It sometimes happens just before someone tries to _____ their own _____.

美剧与美国社会文化

NASA official: You think he could have been trying to _____ _____? And what changed his mind at the last second and ejected?

Foster: It's a possibility, but I'll need to assess his _____ state prior to the crash. Do you have any old videotape of him?

NASA official: We're the _____ government. We _____ everything.

Task 3 Translate the following lines into English, pay special attention to the parts in color, and then watch the video clip and check.

1. 我曾跟他开玩笑说我是他的第二任妻子。他的初恋是NASA,一直都是。
   _____.

2. 他最近压力很大,但他处理得很好。
   _____

3. X-48飞行员位置的竞争真的很激烈。这对我们全家而言都很有压力,但我们撑过来了。
   _____
   _____

4. 是的,当她谈到压力时说漏嘴了。
   _____

5. NASA不是每几个月就给飞行员做药检吗?
   _____

Section B Language Output

Watch video clips in this section, and then choose one clip to dub or role play.

Clip 1: Markov—Dr. Foster—Loker

Clip 2: Dr. Foster—Hilary; Dr. Foster—Loker

Clip 3: Markov—Loker—NASA official—Dr. Foster—Hilary

Words and Expressions

Words related to a shuttle

Telemetry	[təˈlemətri]	n.	遥感勘测
throttle	[ˈθrɔtəl]	n.	油门杆
scramjet	[ˈskræmˌdʒet]	n.	超音速冲压喷射发动机
afterburner		n.	喷射引擎等的再燃装置
CAVU			(航空专业名词)能见度极好
ignition	[igˈniʃən]	n.	点火,着火
mach	[mɑːk]	n.	马赫(音速单位)

Unit 2　Depression

Words

shuttle	[ˈʃʌtl]	n.	航天飞机
scrap	[skræp]	adj.	废弃的
commander	[kəˈmɑːndə]	n.	指挥官,中校
exemplary	[igˈzempləri]	adj.	模范的,典范的
instructor	[inˈstrʌktə]	n.	指导者
cruising	[ˈkruːziŋ]	adj.	巡航的
malfunction	[mælˈfʌŋkʃən]	n.	故障
flap	[flæp]	v.	拍翅(或振翼)飞行
eject	[iˈdʒekt]	v.	喷射,喷出
dove	[dʌv]	v.	(dive的过去式)俯冲
disorient	[disˈɔːrient]	vt.	使……失去方向感
defect	[diˈfekt]	vi.	叛逃
parachute	[ˈpærəʃuːt]	n.	降落伞
pending	[ˈpendiŋ]	prep./ adj.	直到
altitude	[ˈæltitjuːd]	n.	高度;海拔
visibility	[ˌvizəˈbiləti]	n.	能见度
fuzzy	[ˈfʌzi]	adj.	模糊的
punch	[pʌntʃ]	v.	冲
deflection	[diˈflekʃən]	n.	引开;转移
spontaneous	[spɔnˈteiniəs]	adj.	不由自主的,无意识的
hysterical	[hisˈterikəl]	adj.	歇斯底里的
blackout	[ˈblækˌaut]	n.	昏厥
tease	[tiːz]	v.	戏弄,逗弄
demeanor	[diˈmiːnə]	n.	行为;态度;举止
slot	[slɔt]	n.	空位
false start			不成功的开始
narcotic	[nɑːˈkɔtik]	n.	麻醉药品
screen	[skriːn]	v.	甄别;筛选
anti-anxiety		n.	抗焦虑
medication	[ˌmediˈkeiʃən]	n.	治疗药物
withdrawal	[wiðˈdrɔːəl]	n.	戒毒
symptom	[ˈsimptəm]	n.	症状
suicidal	[ˌsuːəˈsaidəl]	adj.	自杀的
impulse	[ˈimpʌls]	n.	冲动

美剧与美国社会文化

tox	[tɔks]	n.	毒药；毒理学
panel	[ˈpænəl]	n.	专门问题小组
positive	[ˈpɔzətiv]	adj.	阳性的
self-medicate		v.	不遵医嘱，自我治疗
dizziness	[ˈdizinis]	n.	头昏眼花
pricey	[ˈpraisi]	adj.	昂贵的
dose	[dəus]	v.	(按剂量)给……服(药)
drug	[drʌg]	v.	下药，把毒药(或麻醉剂)搀入(酒、饮料或食物等)
commence	[kəˈmens]	n.	开始
simulation	[ˌsimjuˈleiʃən]	n.	模拟
footage	[ˈfutidʒ]	n.	镜头
trial	[ˈtraiəl]	n.	审讯
scorn	[skɔːn]	n.	不屑，轻蔑
contempt	[kənˈtempt]	n.	轻视，轻蔑
universal	[ˌjuːniˈvəːsəl]	adj.	普遍的

Phrases

leave up: 任(某物)悬挂着或摆放着，这里指放着不管。

Proper Names

NASA (National Aeronautics and Space Administration): 美国航空航天局
USSR (Union of Soviet Socialist Republics): 简称苏联
Kato Kaelin: 人名，曾与辛普森前妻有暧昧关系
Current Affair: 时事(此处是一电视节目名称)
Duran Duran: 乐队名称

Part III Culture and Society Focus

What makes David Markov anxious and depressed?
What does his wife do to help him?
Is the measure she has taken helpful?

Unit 2   Depression

Depression
What Is Depression? **Statistics about Depression** **Causes of Depression** **Symptoms** **Treatment** **Helping Someone Who Is Depressed** **Depression among College Students**

What Is Depression?

Everyone feels blue or sad now and then, but these feelings don't usually last long and pass within a couple of days. When a person has depression, it interferes with daily life and normal functioning, and causes pain for both the person with depression and those who care about him or her. Doctors call this condition "depressive disorder," or "clinical depression."

Depression is a common mental disorder which adversely affects a person's family, work or school life, and general health.

Depression occurs in persons of all genders, ages, and backgrounds.

Statistics about Depression

According to the World Health Organization (WHO):
- Depression is among the leading causes of disability worldwide, affecting 121 million people around the globe. It's expected that by 2020 it will be the leading global disease burden.
- In the United States alone, estimates for those diagnosed with the disease range from 17 to 21 million people a year or roughly 10 percent of the country.

  In US nearly 2.5 percent of children suffer from depression.

  In US nearly 8.3 percent of adolescents suffer from depression.
- Rates can vary by region, with as little as 5 percent of South and East Asians suffering from depression, and as many as 25 percent of the population suffering from it in Eastern European and former Soviet countries.
- Fewer than 25 % of those affected have access to effective treatments.

Information from Wiki:

In US, around 3.4% of people with major depression commit suicide, and up to 60% of people who commit suicide had depression or another mood disorder.

In China:

According to the statistics provided by the government in 2007, there are about 30 million

Chinese diagnosed as clinical depression. A newly published global medical research indicates that about 1 million people commit suicide all over the world every year. Among these people, 30% are Chinese. Committing suicide is the number one factor leading to death among young people aged from 15 — 34, and among whom depressed people account for 60% — 70%.

Causes of Depression

The mechanism of depression is not known precisely, but it is probably a disturbance of chemical in the brain, causing a biological disorder of mood and mental and physical functions.

Proposed causes include psychological, psycho-social, hereditary, and biological factors.

The following are the possible detailed causes of depression:

- **Biological factors:** Vitamin B12 deficiency, stroke, head injury, the consumption of drugs or alcohol, overwork, lack of sleep, long-term drug use
- **Psychological factors:** neurotic personality structure, low self-esteem and self-defeating or distorted thinking,
- **Psycho-social factors:** the frustrating experiences, loneliness, poverty and social isolation, child abuse (physical, emotional, sexual, or neglect)
- **Hereditary factors:** family history of depression

Symptoms

The symptoms of depression include:

- low mood
- feeling restless and agitated
- weak in concentration
- avoiding friends
- loss of interest in activities that they enjoy
- lack of energy
- guilty feeling
- harder to make decisions
- loss of appetite and weight
- bad performance at work or study
- difficulties in home and family life
- loss of self confidence
- trouble in sleeping
- self-harm, thought about suicide

Treatment

The good news is that statistics reveal that more than 50% of people with depression do recover. However, fewer than 25% of those affected (in some countries fewer than 10%) receive such treatments. Barriers to effective care include the lack of resources, lack of trained providers, and the social stigma associated with mental disorders including depression. It is definitely worthwhile to seek treatment early because the longer depression goes untreated, the harder it is to treat.

Major types of treatments are as follows.

- Antidepressant medicine
- Psychotherapy

Unit 2 Depression

● Antidepressant medicine combined with psychotherapy

Other treatments include electroconvulsive therapy (ECT), light Therapy, cognitive-behavioral therapy, acupuncture, aromatherapy etc.

Antidepressant medications and brief, structured forms of psychotherapy are effective for 60 % — 80 % of those affected. However, like all medicines, antidepressants have some side effects such as dry mouth, dizziness, sleepiness, weight gain/loss, restlessness, trouble sleeping etc. For the most part, drugs and intensive medical therapies are only necessary for severe or persistent cases of depression.

In addition to psychotherapy, a variety of natural methods have been shown to reduce symptoms of depression and restore brain chemistry to appropriate function, therefore, if you suffer from a mild form of depression, you can try the following natural methods:

● Exercises or Yoga
● Diet and Depression Massage Therapy
● Relaxations or Deep Breathing
● Meditation or Prayer

Helping Someone Who Is Depressed

● Listen to them but try not to judge them. Don't offer advice unless they ask for it. If you can see the problem behind the depression, you can help the person to find a solution.
● Spend time with them, listen to their problems and encourage them to keep going with activities in their routine.
● If they're getting worse, encourage them to visit their doctor and get help.

Depression among College Students

<u>In USA:</u>

A growing number of studies are focusing on the rising number of college students diagnosed with depression and other emotional conditions.

According to the International Association of Counseling Services' 2010 National Survey of Counseling Center Directors, 91 percent of the more than 300 counseling center directors surveyed reported seeing an increase in numbers of students with psychological problems over the past year, reports the *Chicago Tribune*.

<u>In China:</u>

In the first 4 months in 2012, 9 college students were reported to having committed suicide in Beijing. Experts point out that among college students who committed suicide, about 60% suffered mental diseases like depression. Depression has become No.1 killer in colleges.

美剧与美国社会文化

Task 1　Warm up

What negative emotions have you experienced in the past two weeks including today? Put a tick beside it.

stressed		great pressure		fear		cynical	
depressed		aimless		anger		disappointed	
helpless		worried		at a loss		nervous	
frustrated		lonely		feeling empty		anxious	

What are likely to be the causes of your negative emotions? Put a tick beside it.

exams		no clear goal		financial difficulty		fierce competition	
illness		worry about future		lack confidence / insecure		poor school facilities	
lack friends		boring college life		not enough sleep		game addiction	
love affairs		tight schedule /too much homework		not able to control myself		relationship with people	
unfair society		problems in study		too much expection from parents		poor family background	

Task 2　Survey and presentation

Step 1　Get the statistics

Count the number of students ticking each negative emotion and each possible cause within your group, add up the numbers of all the groups, and finally get the total number of the whole class. Write the number beside the negative emotions and possible causes in the above tables.

Step 2　Analyze and prepare

Based on the statistics, find out the 3 leading negative emotions and 3 leading causes of the negative emotions with your group members; and discuss about ways to solve the problems. Based on this outline, prepare an oral presentation on "Psychological Problems among College Students."

Rank	1	2	3
Negative emotions			
Causes			
Ways to solve the problems			

Unit 2   Depression

Step 3   Rehearse

Pair work: Practice doing a presentation with your neighbor, and help each other to improve.

Step 4   Present

Present on "Psychological Problems among College Students" as directed in step 2 in class.

Listener task: Take notes about constructive solutions.

Part IV   Writing

Based on the above discussion, write about "Psychological Problems among College Students." You should write at least 200 words, and base your composition on the outline given below:

1. psychological problems of college students
2. possible causes of these problems
3. solutions

Functional Sentence Patterns

Introducing a Topic (II)
- ...has always aroused the greatest concern.
- what impresses us most is ...
- ...has been brought into focus.
- Currently, the issue of ...has been brought to public attention.

Additional Information

Lie to Me is an American television series that originally ran on the Fox network from January 21, 2009 to January 31, 2011. In the show, Dr. Cal Lightman (Tim Roth) and his colleagues in The Lightman Group accept assignments from third parties (commonly local and federal law enforcement), and assist in investigations, reaching the truth through applied psychology: interpreting microexpressions, through the Facial Action Coding System, and body language.

Awards and nominations

Primetime Emmy Awards

● 2009 Primetime Emmy Award for Outstanding Main Title Design (nominee)

People's Choice Awards

Lie to Me was nominated for two awards at the 37th People's Choice Awards and won both of them.

● 2011 Favorite TV Crime Drama (WON)

● 2011 Favorite TV Crime Fighter (Tim Roth, WON)

Characters
Dr. Cal Lightman (Tim Roth) is a psychologist with an expertise in body language and especially microexpressions, and founder of The Lightman Group. This character is based on Dr. Paul Ekman; notable psychologist and expert on body language and facial expressions at UC San Francisco.
Dr. Gillian Foster (Kelli Williams), Dr. Lightman's colleague and co-worker in The Lightman Group. This character is based on Prof. Maureen O'Sullivan, a psychology professor at the University of San Francisco.
Eli Loker (Brendan Hines), an employee of The Lightman Group. Loker is academically educated and has acquired his skills in "reading" people through practice.

Unit 3

Aging

In this unit, you will:
- watch video clips from *Desperate Housewives*;
- understand the lines from it;
- know something about *aging and aging society*;
- learn some expressions on *listing different opinions and giving reasons*.

Section A   Character Introduction

Background: *The day before, Lynette offended Alison by saying that Alison devoted herself to her family only to find that her husband had an affair and left her.*

Do you know how these people are related? Watch the video clip now!

美剧与美国社会文化

This video clip features several characters, what more do you know about them?

Lynette: _____

Tom: _____

Alison: _____

Section B　Story Retelling

Watch the video clip again, then work in pairs and retell the story with the help of the following questions.

1. Why did Alison come to live with Tom and Lynette?

   _____

2. What was Lynette worried about?

   _____

3. What did Tom think of Lynette's worry?

   _____

4. What happened on Halloween night?

   _____

5. What was Tom's final decision? And was Alison happy to accept Tom's decision?

   _____

Part II　Language Appreciation

Section A　Language Input

Task 1　Translate the following lines into English, pay special attention to the parts in color, and then watch the video clip and check.

1. 如果我做得过分了点儿,我很抱歉。

   _____.

2. 我就是不明白你为什么会愿意放弃这一切非要出去工作呢?

   _____.

3. 我就是这样的人。

   _____.

Task 2　Watch video clip 2 twice and fill in the missing words.

Tom:　　You Okay? What time is it?

Lynette:　_____. I'm sorry to wake you up, but I'm _____ _____ your mom. I don't think she's all there.

26

Unit 3 Aging

Tom: You woke me up at 4 a.m. to _____ _____ my mom? You couldn't do that during _____ _____?

Lynette: No, listen, she sent me out to _____ _____ _____, when she already had ten jars. She forgot to wake up the baby.

Tom: She's older, she _____ _____ _____.

Lynette: No, she also has these... _____ mood swings. I mean, today, she almost took my head off for no reason.

Tom: Well, she's...

Lynette: And then, and then she looks like she was gonna _____ _____ tears.

Tom: She's away from home. She isn't used to all this chaos.

Lynette: Okay. I get it. She's your mom, and you love her. And you can _____ _____ _____ for every one of these things. But I think there's more _____ _____ here than just being a little _____. ...Your light's on.

Task 3   Watch video clip 3, and get the English expressions for the following Chinese phrases or sentences:

等一下	
走错方向	
灯灭了	
那里肯定有	
放开我	
我头脑一时发热	

Section B Language Output

Watch video clips in this section, and then choose one clip to dub or role play.

Clip 1: In the kitchen: Lynette—Alison

Clip 2: In the kitchen: Lynette—Tom

Clip 3: In front of Carlos' house: Lynette—Alison

Clip 4: In front of Tom's house: Tom—Alison

美剧与美国社会文化

Words and Expressions

Words

crack	[kræk]	v.	（使……）开裂，破裂
bitch	[bitʃ]	vi.	埋怨，抱怨
jar	[dʒɑː]	n.	罐子，广口瓶
intense	[inˈtens]	adj.	强烈的，剧烈的
swing	[swiŋ]	n.	摆动，摇摆；显著的变化
head	[hed]	vi.	前往
chaos	[ˈkeiɔs]	n.	混乱，紊乱
scattered	[ˈskætəd]	adj.	分散的；糊涂的
worrywart	[ˈwʌriwɔːt]	n.	自寻烦恼的人
hurricane	[ˈhʌrikən]	n.	飓风
counselor	[ˈkaunsələ]	n.	顾问，参事；（儿童夏令营）管理员
dementia	[diˈmenʃiə]	n.	痴呆
senile	[ˈsiːnail]	adj.	衰老的
tactic	[ˈtæktik]	n.	方法，策略；手段
costume	[ˈkɔstjuːm]	n.	（戏剧或电影的）戏装，服装；（某地或某历史时期的）服装，装束
veteran	[ˈvetərən]	n.	经验丰富的人；老兵
backup	[ˈbækˌʌp]	n.	备用品，后备
cupboard	[ˈkʌbəd]	n.	壁橱
stash	[stæʃ]	n.	藏匿处，隐藏处
therapy	[ˈθerəpi]	n.	治疗，疗法
load	[ləud]	vt.	把……装上车[船]

Phrases and Idioms

cross the line:

1) to change from being acceptable to being unacceptable

—I thought the jokes crossed the line and were basically embarrassing.

2) to do something wrong

—If you steal someone's idea, you have absolutely crossed the line.

hang on: to wait awhile

—Hang on a minute. I need to talk to you.

Unit 3   Aging

Proper Names

the nursing home 护理院,养老院

Part III   Culture and Society Focus

Section A   Festival

Watch the video clip, what festival are they celebrating? How do you know? Fill in the following chart.

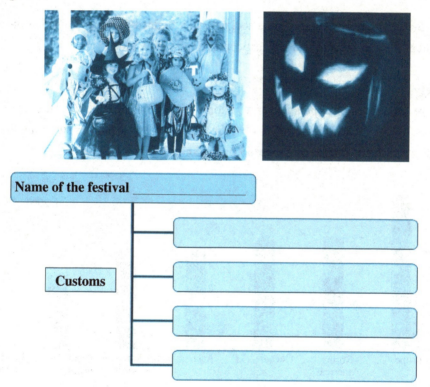

Name of the festival _____

Customs

Section B   Aging

- When Alison, Tom's mother, came back to her son's house, she said "so nice to feel useful again." What are the reasons for her sense of uselessness?
- What are the symptoms of "sundowning," the disease that Tom's mother suffers from?

29

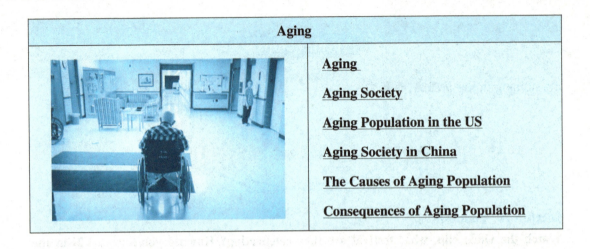

Aging
Aging
Aging Society
Aging Population in the US
Aging Society in China
The Causes of Aging Population
Consequences of Aging Population

Aging

Aging (*British English*, ageing) can be sociologically defined as the combination of physical, psychological and social process that affects people as they grow older.

Aging Society

When the proportion of population of a region over aged 65 reaches 7%, the region enters "aging society." From the chart below, it is obvious that "elder explosion" is sweeping the world.

Figure 1   Proportion of population over 65 by regions, 2000 and 2050.

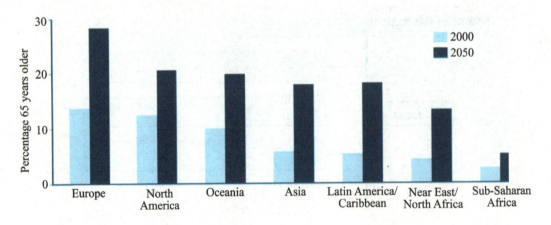

[Source: U.S. Bureau of the Census (2000)]

Aging Population in the US

USA is one of the countries with the highest birth rate and population growth among the developed countries. With 17.4% population over 65 years old in 2010, American society, which has stepped into an aging society since the 1940s, is a typical aging society today.

Unit 3 Aging

Age	2000	2050	% change
Total	275.306	403.687	46.6
16—64	177.974	236.602	32.9
65+	34.835	81.999	135.4
85+	4.312	19.352	349.8

Table 1 Population of the US, by age, 2000 and 2050 (in millions)
〔Source: US Bureau of the Census〕

Between 2000 and 2050, the number of older people above 65 is projected to increase by 135%. Moreover, the population aged 85 and over, which is the group most likely to need health and long-term care services, is projected to increase by 350%. Over this time period, the proportion of the population that is over the age of 65 will increase from 12.7% in 2000 to 20.3% in 2050; the proportion of the population that is aged 85 and older will increase from 1.6% in 2000 to 4.8% in 2050.

Post-retirement Income Sources

Generally speaking, the American retirees' income comes from the following sources:
- Social Security benefits
- Company pension
- 401(k) retirement plan
- Personal investments

Post-retirement Lifestyles

American retirees can choose to live independently, in a senior apartment or in a nursing home, which depend on their health and financial conditions.

Aging Society in China

In 2010, the National Bureau of Statistics of China publicized the main data of the sixth national population census, which found that more than 7 percent of total people are older than 65 years old in 26 provinces in China, and China has become an aging society.

The Causes of Aging Population

Two factors contribute to it: one is that the rate of birth is falling historically and the other is that improved medical technology and health awareness are allowing us to live longer lives.

Consequences of Aging Population

Rising aging population not only means fewer labor force in the labor market, but also it challenges the current health care system, social security system and system of nursing the elderly.

Measures Taken by the USA Government

The aging of population can have severe impact on economical and social development, hence, American government has taken some measures.

— Make laws and special policies to protect the elders' legitimate rights and interests; set up institutions to serve the aging population, including the Administration on Aging (AOA), Counsel Committee on Aging and US Social Security Administration Office.

— Set up and improve its social security system on aging.

— Set up and improve its service network for the elder.

— Provide more financial support by the government.

— Encourage birth and keep a relatively moderate birth rate, 2.1.

— Attract young immigrants.

Task 1　Warm up

Fill in the following table.

Imagine you are in 2050. What would be happening to you?

In 2050	What do you think about...	Probable	It depends	Impossible
Your age:	Going backing to work after retiring?			
Your mother's age:	Helping to nurse your grandchild (ren)?			
Your father's age:	Living with your parents?			
Your child(ren)'s age:	Sending your parents to Elderly Social Center?			

Task 2　As China is also becoming an aging society, have you ever figured out some way-outs? Make a presentation on this problem from the aspects of individuals and the government respectively.

Unit 3 Aging

Step 1 Brainstorm some solutions both for individuals and the government.

Join insurance scheme

Step 2 Prepare

Make an outline.

Introduction: Briefly state the problem.

Body: (Refer to step 1 and give your one or two solutions and explain why some specific measures should be taken.)

Conclusion: (Stress the importance and urgency of the issue.)

Useful Expressions	Your Own Word Box
God helps those who help themselves. Save up for a rainy day. There is no easy method, but ... might be some help. Only and lonely	

Step 3　Rehearse

Practice your presentation with a classmate.

Listener task: Is your partner's solution practical and feasible?

Step 4　Present

Present it to the whole class.

Listener task: Listen carefully to the reasons to take some measures and decide what measures are the most urgent to be taken.

Part IV　Writing

Write about the following topic:

　　The population of China is graying. Some people think that it is time to delay retirement age. Others believe that it is still too early to do so.

　　Discuss both these views and give your own opinion.

　　Give reasons for your answer and include any relevant examples.

　　Write at least 200 words.

Functional Sentence Patterns

To list different views:

... as opposed to the above opinion,

... stand in a different ground.

... hold a different opinion.

To give reasons:

The underlying reasons for it might be ...

... be accountable for ...

... add up to ...

Unit 3　Aging

Additional Information

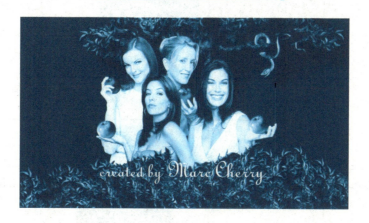

	Desperate Housewives		
Genre	Comedy-drama Mystery		
Created by	Marc Cherry		
Starring	**Actress**	**Picture of the Actress**	**Character**
	Teri Hatcher		Susan Mayer
	Felicity Huffman		Lynette Scavo

(continuing)

	Marcia Cross		Bree Van De Kamp
	Eva Longoria		Gabrielle Solis
No. of seasons	8		
No. of episodes	166		
Broadcast			
Original channel	ABC		
Original run	October 3, 2004—2011		

Unit 4

Gender and Love

In this unit, you will:
- watch video clips from *Ugly Betty*;
- understand the lines from the clips;
- know something about *homosexuality*;
- learn some expressions on *listing different opinions and arguments*.

Part I Story Exploration

Section A Character Introduction

Background: *Marc's mother visits the office of Mode and stops at the desk to see Amanda. Daniel and Alexis are brothers, but Alexis is a transsexual now. And they are competing for the position of editor-in-chief of the Mode Magazine.*

Do you know how these people are related? Watch the video clip now!

美剧与美国社会文化

This video clip features two characters, what more do you know about them?

Marc: _____

Betty: _____

Section B Story Retelling

Watch the video clip again, then work in pairs and retell the story with the help of the following information.

Scene	Characters	Key words
In the office	Mrs. Weiner Amanda Marc Betty	break one's heart drug and sex addiction Marc's new girlfriend before Betty is able to mention kiss
In the bathroom	Marc Betty Amanda	beg play tell Marc and Betty the dinner plans
In Betty's household	Marc—Betty	intense Betty's room tell the truth
	Marc—Betty	in the kitchen need not worry about the letter run to notify Daniel
	Mrs. Weiner—Marc	gather their things to leave criticize no interest in knowing
	Marc—Betty	back home on her front porch learn a lot about family

Part II Language Appreciation

Section A Language Input

Task 1 Watch the video clip twice and fill in the missing information.

Marc: Mom!
Mrs.Weiner: There's my Marcy boy!
Marc: Hi! Mwah. Mwah. Mwah. Mwah. I thought you were going to the _____, and then we were going to dinner.
Mrs.Weiner: Sweetie, I had a catastrophe. Lady Buttons of Camelot lost a jewel on her collar. That's a 10-point _____ for appearance. Can you have one of your fashion people here fix it?
Marc: Oh, of course. Um, fashion person. Help!
Amanda: I would be happy to. I just hope my drug and sex addictions don't _____ _____ _____ _____.
Marc: Oh, mom...why don't you go down to the cafeteria and get some lunch, and I'll bring the collar to you?
Amanda: Wait, Marc. _____ _____ _____ introduce your mom to your new lady love? The one in whose bosom you found comfort after dating a skunk like me.
Mrs.Weiner: You're _____ _____ _____?
Amanda: Oh, look, and here she is. This is Marc's new girlfriend, Betty.
Betty: Girlfriend? That's a good one, Amanda.
Mrs.Weiner: Well, what's so funny?
Betty: Well, you know, because Marc's ...
Betty: You haven't told your mom you're _____? I mean, isn't it a little... I don't know, I—just—just that you're so...sparkly!
Marc: She visits twice a year. She sees what _____ _____ _____ _____. I can't believe I'm asking you this. I need your help.
Betty: You need my help? Hmm. The girl you've tortured for the last six months?
Marc: I think "tortured" is a little _____.
Betty: Well, my second day here, you tricked me into eating glue by telling me it was white chocolate. No! I _____ _____.
Marc: Oh, I only let you eat two pieces. Come on, Betty! It would really mean a lot to my mother.

美剧与美国社会文化

Task 2 Watch the video clip, and get the English expressions for the following Chinese phrases or sentences.

有机会赢	
闲聊	
某人不会介意吗？	
和……约会	
帮助……摆脱困境	

Task 3 Translate the following lines into English, pay special attention to the parts in color, and then watch the video clip and check.

1. 是我的错。猫咪太缠人了。我不能把她一个人留在酒店。
   _____.

2. 我抹掉了她的头衔。她现在的名字只是Buttons了。
   _____.

3. 她决不会错过这场好戏。
   _____.

Section B

Watch video clips in this section, then choose one clip to dub or role play.

Clip 1: Mrs. Weiner—Amanda—Marc—Betty
Clip 2: Mrs. Weiner—Amanda—Marc—Betty
Clip 3: Marc—Betty in Betty's room
Clip 4: Marc—Mrs. Weiner in Betty's household
Clip 5: Marc—Betty on the porch

Words and Expressions

Words

indiscretion	[ˌɪndɪˈskreʃən]	n.	不检点
drug	[drʌg]	n.	毒品
addiction	[əˈdɪkʃən]	n.	上瘾
catastrophe	[kəˈtæstrəfi]	n.	灾难
collar	[ˈkɔlə]	n.	项圈；衣领
penalty	[ˈpenəlti]	n.	惩罚

Unit 4　Gender and Love

cafeteria	[ˌkæfiˈtiəriə]	n.	自助餐厅
bosom	[ˈbuzəm]	n.	胸怀
skunk	[skʌŋk]	n.	讨厌的人
sparkly	[ˈspɑːkli]	adj.	耀眼的
torture	[ˈtɔːtʃə]	n.	折磨
glue	[gluː]	n.	胶水
ring	[riŋ]	n.	竞技场
cranky	[ˈkræŋki]	adj.	发疯似的
clown	[klaun]	n.	小丑
ruin	[ˈruin]	v.	摧毁
meat loaf			烤肉卷
tragic	[ˈtrædʒik]	adj.	悲惨的,悲剧的
		n.	(文艺作品或生活中的)悲剧因素,悲剧风格
counsel	[ˈkaunsəl]	v.	咨询
weird	[wiəd]	adj.	怪异的
swishy	[ˈswiʃi]	adj.	娘娘腔的
out	[aut]	v.	暴露
original	[əˈridʒənl]	adj.	原创的;新颖的;最初的
freaking	[friːkiŋ]	adj.	令人惊异的
fabulous	[ˈfæbjuləs]	adj.	极好的

Phrases and Idioms

knock up

1) (Chiefly American slang) to make pregnant 使女人怀孕

　— "You think you can knock up my daughter and not marry her?"

2) (Chiefly British) to wear out; exhaust 使筋疲力尽

　— The long journey really knocked me up.

strip away: to remove or peel something from someone or something 除去

　— Carefully stripping away centuries of paint, the scientists uncovered a valuable old wall painting.

show up: to appear; to arrive 出现

　— We waited all day and he never showed up.

turn the moustache upside down: to calm down 平静下来

　Marc: My family is not your family, so let's turn that moustache upside down and go downstairs and finish dinner and then we'll be out of here.

Part III Culture and Society Focus

- In this video clip Marc asks Betty to act as his girlfriend, why does he do that?
- When Marc's mother knows the truth, what's her reaction?

HOMOSEXUALITY

Sexual Orientation and Homosexuality
Number of Homosexuals in the United States
Homosexuals in China
Causes for Homosexuality: Nature or Nurture
Attitudes toward Homosexuality
Support for Legal Gay Relations Hits New High

IT FEELS SO RIGHT FOR ME, WHY SHOULD IT BOTHER SOMEONE ELSE?

Sexual Orientation and Homosexuality

Sexual orientation refers to an enduring pattern of emotional, romantic, and/or sexual attractions to men, women, or both sexes. Sexual orientation is usually discussed in terms of three categories:

- ■ Heterosexual or straight—having emotional, romantic, or sexual attractions to members of the other sex (the most commonly found sexual orientation in all cultures).
- ■ Homosexual or gay—having emotional, romantic, or sexual attractions to members of one's own sex (Gay women are also called lesbians).
- ■ Bisexual—having emotional, romantic, or sexual attractions to both men and women.

Number of Homosexuals in the United States

According to the Williams Institute at the UCLA School of Law (a sexual orientation law and public policy think tank), 9 million (about 3.8%) of Americans identify as gay, lesbian, bisexual or transgender (2011). The institute also found that bisexuals make up 1.8% of the population, 1.7% are gay or lesbian and transgender adults make up 0.3% of the population.

However, the number of LGBT persons in the U.S. is subjective. The most widely accepted statistic is that 1 in every 10 individuals is LGBT; while some research estimates 1 in 20. A variety of reasons may account for the difficulty in a reliable estimation of the number of LGBT people. It may depend on one's definition of gay (which may vary by study) and the participants' willingness to identify as gay, bisexual, lesbian or transgender.

Unit 4　Gender and Love

Homosexuals in China

It is estimated that gay men and women constitute between 1 and 5 percent of the Chinese population, which means there could be as many as 60 million homosexuals in China. According to estimates by Zhang Beichuan, an expert on homosexuality and AIDS at Qingdao University, there are 30 million homosexuals in China, with 20 million of them gay men and the remainder lesbians. [Source: *China Daily*]

Causes for Homosexuality: Nature or Nurture

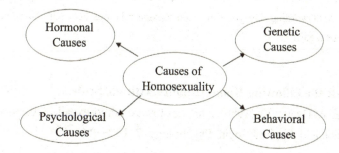

[Source: Adapted from Wolff (1971), Gupta (1996) and Kallman (1952)]

There is no common agreement among scientists about the exact reasons for homosexuality. Although much research has been done about the possible genetic, hormonal, developmental, social, and cultural influences on homosexuality, the debate continues to this day without any conclusive resolution. Many think that homosexuality is not a choice, but rather a complex interplay of nature and nurture (biological and environmental factors).

Attitudes toward Homosexuality

Societal attitudes toward homosexuality vary greatly in different historical periods and different cultures. Throughout recorded history homosexual relationships and acts have mostly been stigmatized around the world. It was ever believed to be chosen sexual behavior, abnormal addiction, sinful activity — hated by God; unnatural, criminal behavior. Even in the 20th century, intense homophobic prejudice against homosexuals was widespread. It is only in recent years that homosexuality has become more tolerated in western society, with some countries passing legislation to recognize homosexual relations and protect the rights of homosexual couples.

Support for Legal Gay Relations Hits New High

According to 2011 Gallup poll, 64% of Americans think gay or lesbian relations between consenting adults should be legal, the highest since it first asked the question more than 30 years ago.

Do you think gay or lesbian relations between consenting adults should or should not be legal?

Note: 1977—2008 wording: Do you think homosexual relations between consenting adults should or should not be legal?
GALLUP

Task 1 Complete the following Homosexuality Attitude Scale.

〔Source: Kite, M.E. & Deaux, K. (1986). Attitudes toward homosexuality: Assessment and behavioral consequences. Basic and Applied Social Psychology, 7, 137—162.〕

Please indicate your level of agreement with the items below using the following scale:

1	2	3	4	5
Strongly Agree	Agree	Neutral	Disagree	Strongly Disagree

Attitude toward Homosexuality	Score
1. I would not mind having a homosexual friend.	
2. Finding out that an artist was gay would have no effect on my appreciation of his/her work.	
3. I would not be afraid for my child to have a homosexual teacher.	
4. I do not really find the thought of homosexual acts disgusting.	
5. I see the gay movement as a positive thing.	
6. Homosexuality, as far as I'm concerned, is not mental illness.	
7. I would not mind being employed by a homosexual.	
8. I would not decline membership in an organization just because it had homosexual members.	
9. I would vote for a homosexual in an election for public office.	

Unit 4 Gender and Love

(continuing)

Attitude toward Homosexuality	Score
10. If I knew someone were gay, I would still go ahead and form a friendship with that individual.	
11. I would not look for a new place to live if I found out my roommate was gay.	
12. Homosexuals are not more likely to commit deviant sexual acts, such as child molestation, rape, and voyeurism (Peeping Toms), than are heterosexuals.	
13. The increasing acceptance of homosexuality in our society is not aiding in the deterioration of morals.	
14. If I were a parent, I could accept my son or daughter being gay.	
TOTAL SCORE	

Task 2 Pair work—create a dialogue on the basis of the situations in the Homosexuality Attitude Scale.

Step 1 Compare your answers with your partner. What ideas do you have in common, and what ideas are different? You can focus on several of the statements from the Homosexuality Attitude Scale and talk about or debate them.

Step 2 Prepare

Make an outline.

| Topic: (e.g. changing school) |
| Roles: (e.g. Emily and Cherry) |
| Situation: (e.g. I would not want my child to have a homosexual teacher. Emily and Cherry meet in the street. Emily complains about her daughter's gay teacher, and she's going to transfer her daughter to a new school.) |
| *Dialogue*
A:
B: |

美剧与美国社会文化

Useful Expressions	Functional Sentence Patterns
chosen, unnatural, abnormal addiction, sinful activity, criminal behavior, mental disorder, perverted, disgusting, speak like a woman, dress like a woman, equal rights, influence on, change from hostility to tolerance, pass laws to protect, deny, keep an open mind	How have you been doing? What a pleasant surprise! Haven't seen you for ages. What's new with you? Can't complain! Can't be worse! Not bad. How about you? You can't believe it! There is no doubt that...

Step 3　Rehearse

Practice your dialogue with your partner.

Step 4　Present

Present it to the whole class.

Listener task: Listen carefully and take notes, which might be helpful in your speaking and writing.

Part IV　Writing

Write about the following topic:

　　Today as more and more homosexuals are coming out of the closet, gay marriage has become a subject that is highly debated and appears to be unsolvable. Some people believe that homosexuals should be given equal rights in the society including the right to marry, while some feel strongly that gay marriage is against the law of nature. What is your view on the subject?

　　Give reasons for your answer and include any relevant examples.

　　Write at least 200 words.

Functional Sentence Patterns

Listing Different Opinions and Arguments

● Nowadays there is a growing concern over...

● Currently, the issue of ...has been brought to public attention.

● There are different opinions among people as to...

Unit 4   Gender and Love

- As far as I am concerned,...
- It is true that..., but it doesn't necessarily mean that...
- Taking all these into consideration, we should...
- It is (high/about) time that something was done about it.

Additional Information

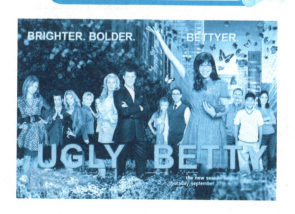

Ugly Betty			
Genre	Comedy-drama		
Created by	Fernando Gaitán		
	Actress	**Picture of the Actress**	**Character**
Starring	America Ferrera		Betty Suarez
	Vanessa L. Williams		Wilhelmina Slater

(continuing)

	Michael Urie		Marc St. James
	Becki Newton		Amanda Tanen
No. of seasons	4		
No. of episodes	85		
Broadcast			
Original channel	ABC		
Original run	September 28, 2006—April 14, 2010		

Unit 5

Nonmarital Pregnancy

In this unit, you will:
- watch video clips from *Lost*;
- understand the lines from it;
- know something about *nonmarital pregnancy*;
- learn some expressions on *giving advice*.

Part I Story Exploration

Section A Character Introduction

What do you know about the following characters? Watch the video clip now and briefly introduce them.

	Thomas
	Claire

美剧与美国社会文化

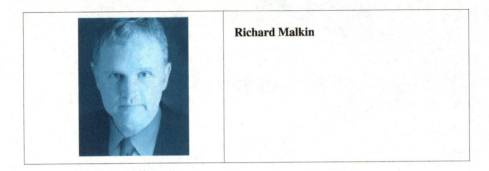

Richard Malkin

Section B Story Retelling

Watch the video clip again, then work in pairs and retell the story with the help of the following key sentences.

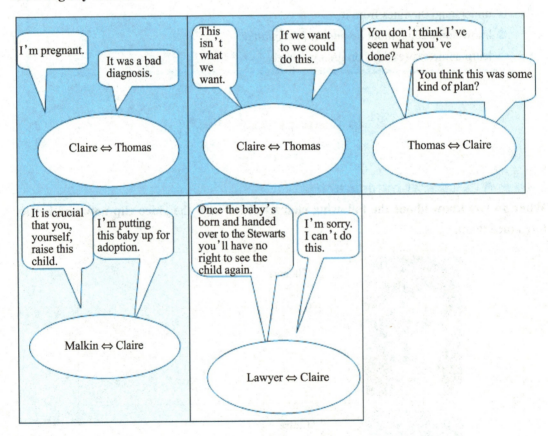

Unit 5 Nonmarital Pregnancy

Part II Language Appreciation

Section A Language Input

Task 1 Watch the video clip twice and fill in the missing information.

[We see Claire coming out of her bathroom with a pregnancy test in her hand.]

Thomas: Is it pink?

Claire: I don't know yet.

Thomas: I mean, did you _____ pee on it?

Claire: I don't know, just give me a second.

Thomas: Maybe you didn't do it right.

Claire: Thomas, I can pee _____ _____ _____.

Thomas: Okay, well what color is it?

Claire: How long's it been?

Thomas: 6 — 66 seconds. Oh god. Okay, it's _____ _____ _____.

Claire: Two pink lines?

Thomas: Pink? No, no, no, these are, like, red.

Claire: What? They're pink.

Thomas: These two lines?

Claire: They're pink.

Thomas: Okay, first of all these _____ are not always _____.

Claire: Thomas. Thomas!

Thomas: No, no, no, my uncle he thought he had testicular cancer, remember that.

Claire: He did. He's dead.

Thomas: Yeah. I mean, no, no. It was like the wrong — it was _____ _____ _____. Look, this thing, it doesn't mean for sure that you're pregnant.

Claire: Thomas — Thomas!

Thomas: We can go get another one.

Claire: I am _____ _____ _____, okay. Six weeks. That never happens. I'm pregnant.

Thomas: Okay. Okay. Look, it's all going to be okay.

Claire: I know. I know.

Thomas: Hey, Claire? If we, if we want to we could do this.

Claire: Stop it.

Thomas: No. I'm not _____.

Claire: My mom would _____ me.

Thomas: She basically has already.

Claire: Yeah. But with what? My _____ _____ _____ _____ job at Fish and Fry?

Thomas: You're not the only one with a job, you know. I mean, I've got my painting.

51

美剧与美国社会文化

Claire: That's sweet, but this isn't what we want.
Thomas: Maybe it is. This could be like, uh, I don't know. It could be like the _____ _____.

Claire: You, you really want to try?
Thomas: Yeah. Claire, I love you.

Task 2 Watch the video clip, and get the English expressions for the following Chinese phrases or sentences.

反应过火	
和……分手	
到底, 究竟; 见鬼	
证明你做的是有道理的	
在服避孕药	
故意的	
发疯的	

Task 3 Translate the following lines into English, pay special attention to the parts in color, and then watch the video clip and check.

1. 这是不是上次你不给我占卜的原因？
_____?

2. 孩子的父亲不会在孩子的生活中，也不会在你的生活中扮演任何角色。
_____.

3. 这孩子不能由你之外的任何人来抚养。
_____.

4. 如果Thomas和我不和好的话，我会把这孩子送去给人领养。
_____.

Section B Language Output

Watch video clips in this section, then choose one clip to dub or role play.
Clip 1: Thomas — Claire
Clip 2: Thomas — Claire
Clip 3: Richard Malkin — Claire
Clip 4: Mr. and Mrs. Stewart — Claire — the lawyer

Unit 5 Nonmarital PREGNANCY

Words and Expressions

Words

pregnant	[ˈpregnənt]	adj.	怀孕的
pink	[piŋk]	adj.	粉红色的
pee	[piː]	n.	小便
		vi.	小便
definitely	[ˈdefinitli; ˈdefənitli]	adv.	肯定地,当然地,明确地
testicular	[tesˈtikjulə]	adj.	睾丸的,双丸状的
cancer	[ˈkænsə]	n.	癌,肿瘤,毒瘤
diagnosis	[daiəgˈnəusis]	n.	诊断
disown	[disˈəun]	v.	否认,声明同……脱离关系
basically	[ˈbeisikəli]	adv.	基本上
drape	[dreip]	n.	布帘
chip	[tʃip]	n.	薯条
over-react			反应过度强烈
abandonment	[əˈbændənmənt]	n.	放弃
crap	[kræp]	n.	<俚>废话;垃圾;粪便
bastard	[ˈbæstəd]	n.	混蛋
justify	[ˈdʒʌstifai]	vt.	替……辩护,证明……是正当的
pill	[pil]	n.	药丸,药片
psychic	[ˈsaikik]	n.	通灵的人
blurry	[ˈbləːri]	adj.	模糊的
crucial	[ˈkruːʃəl]	adj.	决定性的,关键的
parent	[ˈpɛərənt; ˈperənt]	v.	抚养
adoption	[əˈdɔpʃən]	n.	采用,采纳;收养
befall	[biˈfɔːl]	v.	发生;降临
correspond	[ˌkɔrisˈpɔnd]	vi.	符合;相当;通信
discharge	[disˈtʃɑːdʒ]	n.	释放;发射;准许离开;排出物
lullaby	[ˈlʌləˌbai]	n.	摇篮曲,催眠曲

Phrases and Idioms

in the hell: exclamation, used to express anger or to give emphasis "究竟,到底",用于表示愤怒或强调

on the pill: taking a contraceptive pill regularly, esp. every day, in order to prevent a woman from becoming pregnant 在服避孕药

Fish and Fry 煎鱼店
Malkin [ˈmɔːkin] 麦尔肯
Eileen [ˈailiːn] 艾琳(女子名)
Joseph [ˈdʒəuzif; ˈdʒəuzəf] 约瑟夫(男子名)
Melbourne [ˈmelbən] 墨尔本(澳大利亚城市)

Part III Culture and Society Focus

Section A Australian English vs. British English and American English

English is known to be the universal language of today. Although there are many dialects of English, the following are usually used as standard accents: Received Pronunciation for the United Kingdom, General American for the United States, and General Australian for Australia.

These three varieties of English have many similarities, but also a great number of differences. The differences can exist in pronunciation, spelling and grammar. However, the difference in pronunciation is the most remarkable. In American English the "r" at the end of the word almost always affects its pronunciation, whereas in Australian English and British English the "r" is often silent. What's more, in Australian English many words have sounds that are eliminated. Instead of saying good day, Australians say g'day. The main pronunciation difference between the three, however, is the pronunciation of the vowel sounds. (Source: ArticlesBase.com — Free Online Articles Directory)

Australian Vowels

In Australian English vowels tend to be more fronted. The majority of "the Australian accent" is most readily identified by the following six sounds [Mitchel & Delbridge (1965)].

British	→	AusE (IPA)	Example		
/ei/	→	/æi/	Day	→	die
/əu/	→	/ʌu/	Row	→	raow
/iː/	→	/iə/	Me	→	mere
/uː/	→	/əu/	Boot	→	boat
/au/	→	/æu/	Cow	→	caew
/ai/	→	/ɔi/	Nine	→	noy

Unit 5 Nonmarital Pregnancy

Section B

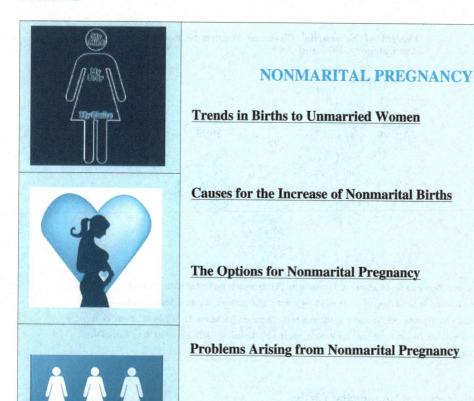

NONMARITAL PREGNANCY

Trends in Births to Unmarried Women

Causes for the Increase of Nonmarital Births

The Options for Nonmarital Pregnancy

Problems Arising from Nonmarital Pregnancy

Public Policy Interventions

● In this video clip, are Thomas and Claire a married couple? How can you tell?
● When Thomas and Claire find out about Claire's pregnancy, what do they do about it?

Trends in Births to Unmarried Women: Four in Ten Children Are Born to Unwed Mothers

In the U.S., nonmarital births are widespread, touching families of varying income class, race, ethnicity, and geographic area. Births to unmarried women have risen dramatically in recent decades. According to the U.S. Census Bureau 2011, the proportion of children born outside marriage in the US has leapt from 10% in 1980 to 40.8% in 2010. This increase in nonmarital childbearing is driven primarily by women in their 20s and 30s opting to have children without getting married (Figure 1).

Figure 1

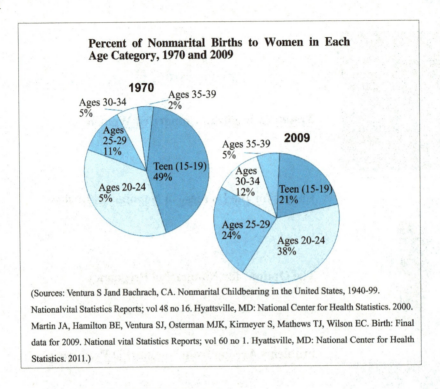

Causes for the Increase of Nonmarital Births

Many factors may have contributed to the upsurge in childbearing outside of marriage. Some analysts attribute this to changed attitudes toward fertility and marriage. Other possible factors include:

- *marriage postponement,*
- *declines in marital fertility,*
- *increases in divorce and separation,*
- *an increase in the number of cohabiting couples,*
- *increased sexual activity outside of marriage,*
- *low levels of contraceptive use,*
- *declining abortion rates,*
- *lack of marriageable partners,*
- *increased wages and levels of employment for women,*
- *Government support for unmarried mothers.*

The Options for Nonmarital Pregnancy

In the event of an unwanted pregnancy, below are common options that are available in various parts of the world to date.

Unit 5 Nonmarital Pregnancy

a) Give birth to the child. After birth, the child could be kept or given up for adoption.

Notes:

- *In 2004, for unmarried women, slightly over half of pregnancies (51%) ended in live birth, an increase from 43% in 1990.*
- *Today more women are keeping their babies — even if they are not married.*
- *The percentage of premarital births placed for adoption has decreased since the 1970s from 8.3% to 2% in the 1990s.*

b) Abortion.

Note: In 2004, for unmarried women, 35% of the pregnancies ended in abortion and 13% ended in fetal loss. Nationwide abortion rates have continued to decline since 1990. (Freundlich, 1998)

c) Donate the embryo to a fertility clinic.

The following figure shows the changes in pregnancy, birth and abortion rates for unmarried women over the period from 1990 to 2006.

Figure 2

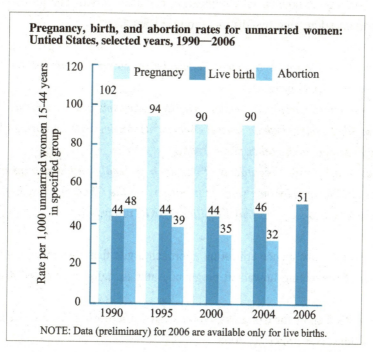

[Source: Ventura, S., Abma, J., Mosher, W.D. & Henshaw, S. (April 14, 2008). Estimated Pregnancy Rates by Outcome for the United States, 1990—2004. National Vital Statistic Reports, 56 (15), 1—26. Accessed from the CDC National Center for Health Statistics Website.]

Problems Arising from Nonmarital Pregnancy

The children of unmarried parents are more likely to:
- *have fewer economic resources,*
- *receive less parenting from their fathers,*
- *do poorly in school,*
- *have emotional and behavioral problems,*
- *become teenage parents,*
- *be seriously abused both sexually and physically.*

It is estimated that in America about 50% of children growing up today will spend some time living with an unmarried, cohabiting couple. Some experts believe that a continuation of the current shift away from marriage would be a disaster for those children.

Public Policy Interventions

In recognition of the potential long-term consequences of nonmarital births, the federal government's strategy to nonmarital childbearing has been varied. The following are the public policy interventions addressing two distinct groups of females:

- *directed at teens, such as abstinence education programs, comprehensive sex education programs, and youth programs;*
- *focused on adults, namely the healthy marriage programs and the responsible fatherhood programs (that usually include several components dealing with improving communication skills with respect to the other parent); and*
- *provided to all persons regardless of age such as family planning programs, adoption services, and federal income support programs — the Child Support Enforcement and Temporary Assistance for Needy Families (TANF) programs.*

Advocates of the abstinence education approach argue that abstinence is the most effective (100%) means of preventing unwanted pregnancy and sexually transmitted diseases (including HIV/AIDS).

〔Source: CRS Report for Congress, Nonmarital Childbearing: Trends, Reasons, and Public Policy Interventions, November 20, 2008〕

Task Make a presentation about your group's advice on premarital sex.
Step 1 Work with your group members and brainstorm reasons to be abstinent.
People choose to be abstinent before marriage for many reasons, work with your group members to brainstorm possible reasons for some people to be abstinent.
- I need to finish my education.

Unit 5 Nonmarital Pregnancy

- I don't want to contract a fatal STI, like HIV.
- _____
- _____
- _____
- _____
- _____
- _____
- _____
- ...

Step 2 Talk with your group members about your reasons to be abstinent.

Which of these reasons are important to you? And why? Please try to give some details.

_____
_____
_____

Step 3 Work with your group members to give advice to a confused friend.

If a friend named Dora came to you for advice on having premarital sex, which reasons would you ask her to think about? The following are your friend's remarks:

"*I am 18 years old. My boyfriend is 20. He often wants to have sex with me. He says he loves me and if I get pregnant, he will marry me. The other night we almost did it. I think I want to, but there is an inner voice telling me not to. What do you think?*"

_____
_____

Useful Expressions	Your Own Word Box
sexually transmitted diseases develop social and behavioral problems a fleeting romance rather than a lasting relationship permanent damage total loss of freedom cut back on social life abandon educational and career goals immense personal sacrifices not worth the gamble set personal limits intimate without having sex attract and marry the right person	

Step 4 Present your group's advice to the class.

Listener task: Listen carefully and take notes, which might be helpful in your speaking and writing.

Part IV Writing

Write about the following topic:

Assume you are an advice columnist for a magazine. Below are some letters that you received this month. Choose one and write a letter of reply.

Dear Cathy,

I am 20, unmarried and pregnant. My boyfriend is 22. Since I became pregnant he started to act very distant. It was he who proposed to have sex in the name of moving up in the relationship. At the beginning, we both felt it was very romantic, but three months later, I was pregnant. I asked him to stay home more since I needed more care, but he went out more with friends and often came home very late. When I called him he seemed so irritable. I feel hurt and scared. What should I do?

Emily

Dear Cathy,

I am 23 years old. My boyfriend is 25. We've been together for about two years. I think we love each other, but he goes out with other girls sometimes. I think if we have a baby he would be more committed to our relationship. But he said he was not ready to be a dad. I'm really confused now. What do you think?

Daisy

Give reasons for your answer and include any relevant examples.
Write at least 200 words.

Functional Sentence Patterns

Giving Advice

- You have asked me for my advice with regard to _____, and I will try to make some conductive suggestions here.
- In my humble opinion, it would be wise for you to ask yourself the following questions before making this decision.
- I hope you will find these proposals useful, and I would be ready to discuss this matter with you to further details.

Unit 5　Nonmarital Pregnancy

Additional Information

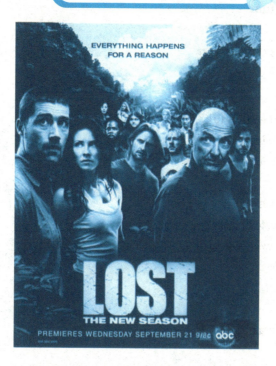

Plot

　　Lost is an American television series that originally aired on ABC from September 22, 2004 to May 23, 2010, consisting of six seasons. *Lost* is a drama series that follows the survivors of the crash of a commercial passenger jet flying between Sydney and Los Angeles, on a mysterious tropical island somewhere in the South Pacific Ocean. The story is told in a heavily serialized manner. Episodes typically feature a primary storyline on the island, as well as a secondary storyline from another point in a character's life.

Awards and nominations

　　A critically acclaimed and popular success, *Lost* was consistently ranked by critics on their lists of top ten series of all time. The first season garnered an average of 15.69 million viewers per episode on ABC. During its sixth and final season, the show averaged over 11 million US viewers per episode. *Lost* was the recipient of hundreds of award nominations throughout its run, and won numerous industry awards, including the Emmy Award for Outstanding Drama Series in 2005, Best American Import at the British Academy Television Awards in 2005, the Golden Globe Award for Best Drama in 2006 and a Screen Actors Guild Award for Outstanding Ensemble in a Drama Series.

美剧与美国社会文化

Fun Time

Please read the following dialogue from the top to the bottom and then from the bottom back to the top and have fun.

BEFORE MARRIAGE

John: Ah ... At last. I can hardly wait!
Jane: Do you want me to leave?
John: No! Don't even think about it.
Jane: Do you love me?
John: Of course! Always have and always will!
Jane: Have you ever cheated on me?
John: No! Why are you even asking?
Jane: Will you kiss me?
John: Every chance I get!
Jane: Will you hit me?
John: Hell no! Are you crazy?!
Jane: Can I trust you?
John: Yes.
Jane: Darling!

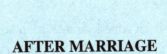

Read from the bottom back to the top.

Unit 6

Voting and Elections

> **In this unit, you will:**
> - watch video clips from *Heroes*;
> - understand the lines from it;
> - know something about the *voting and elections in the United States*;
> - learn some expressions on *how to deliver a speech*.

Section A Character Introduction

Background: *Nathan is going to run for presidency and invites a reporter to have a family brunch together when suddenly Nathan's younger brother Peter came, but Nathan told him it was not the occasion to talk about Linderman.*

Do you know how these people are related? Watch the video clip now!

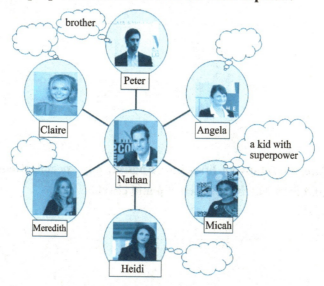

63

美剧与美国社会文化

This video clip features several characters. Please use some words or phrases to describe the following two characters.

Nathan: _____

Claire: _____

Section B Story Retelling

Watch the video clip again, work in pairs, describe each picture with the key words and then reorder them as the main lines of the whole story.

1. What are Nathan and his mother talking about in his office? *Key words: persuade, handle, wire the money, focus on, matter, ruin, run, Congress*	2. Why does the interviewer come to have the family brunch? *Key words: interviewer, family brunch, journal, cover story, not the occasion*
3. Who is the call from? What was the call about? And what was Nathan's response? *Key words: biological mother, a hundred thousand, cover the news, out of wedlock, ruin, running*	4. What is happening to Micah? *Key words: kidnap, superpower, vote, computer*
5. What does Meredith tell Claire about Nathan? *Key words: count on, save her mother, help, money*	6. What is the result of the election campaign? *Key words: win, election, landslide*
7. What does the FBI agent ask Nathan to do? *Key words: FBI, wear a wire, incriminating evidence, put ... behind bars*	8. What does Nathan's mother ask him to do towards his brother's death? *Key words: hide, death, election*

Order: 2, _____, _____, _____, _____, _____, _____, 6

Part II Language Appreciation

Section A Language Input

Task 1 Translate the following lines into English, pay special attention to the parts in color, and then watch the video clip and check.

1. 看来你<u>适应</u>得很好。

_____.

Unit 6　Voting and Elections

2. 我并不是说在我康复期间我没有过低潮。
_____.

3. 看来我们已经重归于好了。
_____.

4. 不论你来是为了什么，现在不是时候。
_____.

5. 那你是说我现在对你而言不够格称为家人了？
_____?

6. 内森抱怨我穿的太随便了。
_____.

Task 2

Watch the video clip of Nathan's speech after he got a landslide twice and fill in the missing information.

　　Thank you all. Thank you very much for your amazing support. A _____. That's what they're calling it. I'm sorry my brother couldn't be with us tonight. But I know that Peter cares about this city more than anyone. You know, our father always said that we had a responsibility to use what God gave us, to help people, to _____ _____ _____ _____ . Pop always made the hard choices for the greater good. He believed in that. And so do I. Our children _____ that. They deserve a better future, a future where they don't have to face their fears alone, but can _____ _____ _____ _____ and find hope. I challenge everyone in here to _____ by example to fight the battle, no matter the cost. Because the world is sick. It's _____ _____ _____ _____. We can help. With our help, it can _____. With our love, with our _____, and with our strength, we can heal it. Let's put aside our differences. Let's _____ our common goals. Let's do it for our children. Let's show them all exactly what we're capable of. Thank you all. Thank you very much. Thank you.

Task 3

Watch the video clip, and get the English expressions for the following Chinese phrases.

自作自受	
得到风声	
跟着	
感情用事	
强硬的外表	
分清事情轻重	
汇钱	

65

美剧与美国社会文化

Section B Language Output

Watch video clips in this section, and then choose one clip to dub or role play.

Clip 1: Nathan—Angela
Clip 2: Micah—Linderman Group
Clip 3: Claire—Meredith

Words and Expressions

Words

brunch	[brʌntʃ]	n.	早午餐
advertise	[ˈædvətaiz]	v.	为……宣传
terrace	[ˈterəs]	n.	阳台
adopt	[əˈdɔpt]	v.	收养
blonde	[blɔnd]	adj.	金色的
run	[rʌn]	v.	竞选
coincidence	[kəuˈinsidəns]	n.	巧合
wedlock	[ˈwedlɔk]	n.	婚姻；婚姻生活
cover	[ˈkʌvə]	v.	掩饰，隐匿
scandal	[ˈskændəl]	n.	丑闻
sperm	[spəːm]	n.	精子
sap	[sæp]	n.	傻瓜
exterior	[eksˈtiəriə; ikˈstiriə]	n.	外表
prioritize	[praiˈɔriˌtaiz]	v.	分清事情轻重
entitled	[inˈtaitld]	adj.	被赋予权力的
snap	[snæp]	v.	用快照拍摄
discretion	[diˈskreʃən]	n.	谨慎，考虑周到
wire	[ˈwaiə]	n.	窃听器
incriminate	[inˈkrimineit]	v.	控告，使负罪
bar	[baː]	n.	法庭
attorney	[əˈtəːni]	n.	律师
precinct	[ˈpriːsiŋkt]	n.	范围，领域；选区
landslide	[ˈlændslaid]	n.	（选举中的）压倒性大胜利
kidnap	[ˈkidnæp]	v.	绑架
accusation	[ˌækjuˈzeiʃən]	n.	诽谤

Unit 6 Voting and Elections

deserve	[diˈzɜːv]	v.	应受,该得
heal	[hiːl]	v.	治疗,治愈
compassion	[kəmˈpæʃən]	n.	同情
inspire	[inˈspaiə(r)]	v.	鼓舞,激励
embrace	[imˈbreis]	v.	拥抱

Phrases and Idioms

figure out: vb. (tr, adverb; may take a clause as object) *informal*

1. to calculate or reckon 算出,想出
   — The boy can't figure out the algebra problems.
2. to understand 理解
   — I can't figure out why he is absent.

give somebody an earful: to tell someone how angry you are with them 辱骂,责骂(某人)
   — He gave me a real earful about being late so often.

get wind of something: to hear a piece of information that someone else was trying to keep secret 得到……风声
   — If anyone gets wind of our plans, we'll be in trouble.

on the heels of something: soon after something 紧跟着,紧接着
   — For Walter, disaster followed hard on the heels of his initial success.

count on: to rely on; to depend on 依靠,依赖
   — That was the only thing they could count on.

be entitled to do: to be furnished with a right or claim to something 有权得到,对某事享有权利
   — If one side failed to honor the contract, the other side should be entitled to cancel it.

out of turn:
1. not in the proper order or sequence 不按次序地
   — No one is allowed to get his ticket out of turn.
2. at an inappropriate time or in an inappropriate manner 不合时宜地
   — Excuse me if I'm talking out of turn, but I feel I must tell you the effect your behavior is having on your father.

Part III Culture and Society Focus

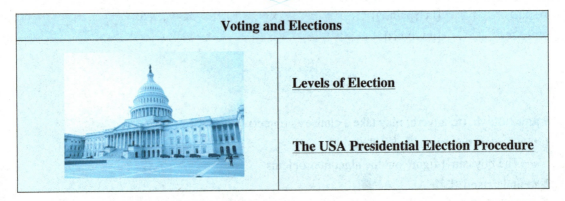

- Which level does Nathan's running in *Heroes* belong to according to the chart 1?
- What is Nathan's approach to win the election campaign?

Levels of Election
Chart 1

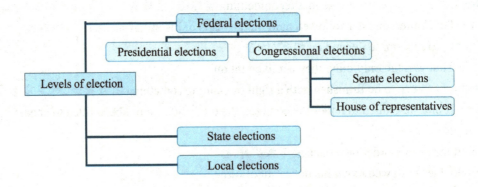

Party System

American politics have been dominated by a two-party system. The two-party system consists of the Democratic Party and the Republican Party. These two parties have won every United States presidential election since 1852 and have controlled the United States Congress since at least 1856.

Unit 6　Voting and Elections

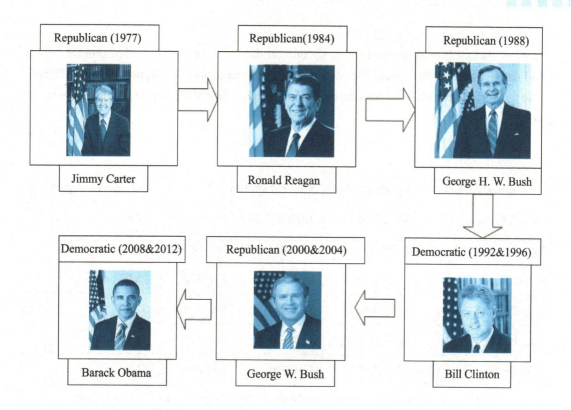

The USA Presidential Election Procedure

　　The election of the President and the Vice President of the United States is an indirect vote in which citizens cast ballots for a slate of members of the U.S. Electoral College; these electors in turn directly elect the President and Vice President. Presidential elections occur every four years on Election Day, the Tuesday between November 2 and 8, coinciding with the general elections of various other federal, states and local races.

Step 1: Primaries and Caucuses

　　The primary elections are run by state and local governments, while the caucuses are organized directly by the political parties. Some states hold only primary elections, some hold only caucuses, and others use a combination of both. In these primaries and caucuses, party members get to vote for the candidate that will represent their party in the upcoming general election.

Step 2: National Conventions

　　At the end of the primaries and caucuses, each party holds a national convention to finalize the selection of one Presidential nominee. During this time, each Presidential candidate chooses a running-mate (or Vice-Presidential candidate).

Step 3: The General (or Popular) Election

Now that each party is represented by one candidate, the general election process begins. Candidates campaign throughout the country in an attempt to win the support of voters. Finally in November, the people vote for one candidate. Without financial support, campaigns can not proceed.

Campaign Finance

Candidate (Party)	Amount raised	Amount spent	Votes	Average spent per vote
Barack Obama (D)	$532,946,511	$513,557,218	69,498,215	$7.39
John McCain (R)	$379,006,485	$346,666,422	59,948,240	$5.78
Ralph Nader (I)	$4,496,180	$4,187,628	738,720	$5.67
Bob Barr (L)	$1,383,681	$1,345,202	523,713	$2.57
Chuck Baldwin (C)	$261,673	$234,309	199,437	$1.17
Cynthia McKinney (G)	$240,130	$238,968	161,680	$1.48

Table 1　Campaign expense by major candidates in United States presidential election, 2008
〔Source: Federal Election Commission〕

When a person casts a vote in the general election, they are not voting directly for an individual Presidential candidate. Instead, voters in each state actually cast their vote for a group of people, known as electors. These electors are part of the Electoral College and are supposed to vote for their state preferred candidate.

Step 4: The Electoral College

In the Electoral College system, each state gets a certain number of electors, based on each state's total number of representation in Congress. Each elector gets one electoral vote. For example, a large state like California gets 54 electoral votes, while Rhode Island gets only four. All together, there are 538 Electoral votes.

In December (following the general election), the electors cast their votes. When the votes are counted on January 6th, the Presidential candidate that gets more than half (270) wins the election. The President-elect and Vice President-elect take the oath of office and are inaugurated two weeks later, on January 20th.

Unit 6　Voting and Elections

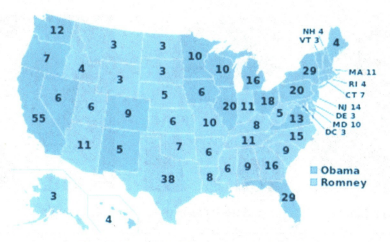

Table 2　Presidential Election Results Map in 2012
(Each number represents the electoral votes a state gave to one candidate.)
〔Source: Wikipedia〕

　　Electoral College map showing the results of the 2012 U.S. presidential election. Incumbent Democratic president Barack Obama won the popular vote in 26 states and Washington, D.C. (denoted in deep blue) to capture 332 electoral votes. Republican challenger Mitt Romney won the popular vote in 24 states (denoted in light blue) to capture 206 electoral votes.

Task 1　Choose the right statements for each president of the U.S. and write down a, b, c... after their names.

　　　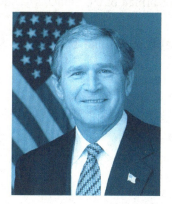　　　

　1. Bill Clinton:　　　2. George W. Bush:　　　3. George Washington:

美剧与美国社会文化

4. Abraham Lincoln: 5. Barack Obama: 6. Franklin D. Roosevelt:

a) the first President of the United States of America, serving from 1789 to 1797
b) famous for his scandals including sexual misconduct
c) successfully led his country through a great constitutional, military and moral crisis — the American Civil War
d) the first African American to hold the office of U.S. president
e) whose father serves as the 41st U.S. president
f) led the United States during a time of worldwide economic crisis and second world war; is the longest serving president in U.S. history

Task 2 Discussion—Making a Public Election Campaign Speech

Suppose you are to run for the chairman of the Students' Union. What public election campaign speech may you deliver?

Step 1 Brainstorm your qualifications and future plans your campaign speech may touch upon.

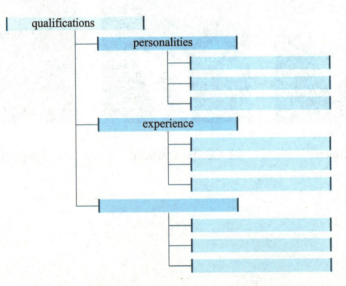

Unit 6 Voting and Elections

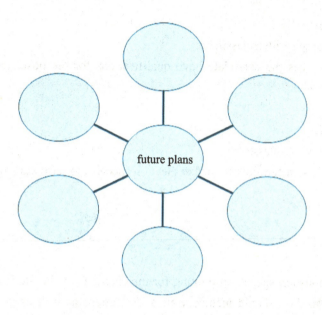

Step 2 Prepare
Make an outline.
Introduction: Beginning the speech

> Opening remarks:
> Purpose and objective:

Body: Developing the speech

> Qualifications:
> Future plans:

Conclusion: Ending the speech

> Summarizing:
> Concluding:
> Ending:

Useful Words and Expressions:
cooperative, highly-motivated, responsible, optimistic, enthusiastic, passionate, outgoing, helpful, curious, ambitious, unyielding, positive, creative, broad-minded, hard-working, sympathetic, honest, enthusiastic, passionate
spirit, perspiration, endurance, perseverance, confidence, positive attitude, self-reliance, inspiration...

Step 3　Rehearse

Practice your speech with a classmate.

Listener task: Does the candidate have qualifications for the post? Do you think his or her future plan is feasible?

Step 4　Practice

Present it to the whole class.

Listener task: Listen carefully to his/her election speech and raise more questions.

Part IV　Writing

Write a campaign speech on running for the chairman of the Students' Union based on the above discussion. You should include your qualifications as well as your future plan. Write at least 200 words.

Functional Sentence Patterns

How to Deliver a Speech

I appreciate the opportunity to be with you today. I am here to ...

Let me start by saying just a few words about ....

I consider it a great honor to be ...

Since I came to the college, I have been holding positions of ....

As a leader of students, I promise to ...

If I am fortunately chosen to be President by you, ...

Additional Information

Unit 6　Voting and Elections

HEROES

Genre	Serial drama /Science fiction
Created by	Tim Kring
Starring	Claire Bennet — Hayden Panettiere Heidi Petrelli—Rena Sofer Nathan Petrelli—Adrian Pasdar Peter Petrelli— Milo Ventimiglia Mohinder Suresh — Sendhil Ramamurthy Angela Petrelli—Cristine Rose
No. of seasons/ episodes	4 / 77
Original channel	NBC
Original run	September 25, 2006 — February 8, 2010

Plot: The first season, known as "Volume One: Genesis," begins as a seemingly ordinary group of people gradually becomes aware that they have special abilities. Events illustrate their reactions to these powers, and how the discovery affects their personal and professional lives. At the same time, several ordinary individuals are investigating the origins and extent of these abilities. Mohinder continues his late father's research into the biological source of the change, while Noah represents a secret organization known only as "the Company." While coping with these new abilities, each of the characters is drawn, willingly or unwillingly, into the Company's conspiracy to control superpowered people and into a race to stop an explosion from destroying New York City.

Unit 7

Terrorism and Prejudices

> **In this unit, you will:**
> - watch video clips from *24*;
> - understand the lines from it;
> - know something about *terrorism*;
> - learn some expressions on *analyzing reasons*.

Part I Story Exploration

Section A Character Introduction

Background: *Los Angeles is under the threat of nuclear bombing.*

Task 1 Watch the video clip, look at the following charts of the characters, and identify the suspected terrorists. Write T for "terrorist," A for "anti-terrorist," and NG for "information not given."

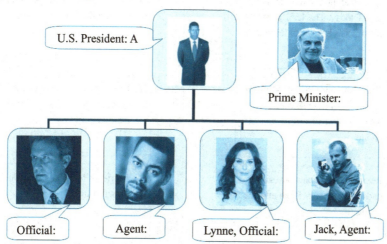

美剧与美国社会文化

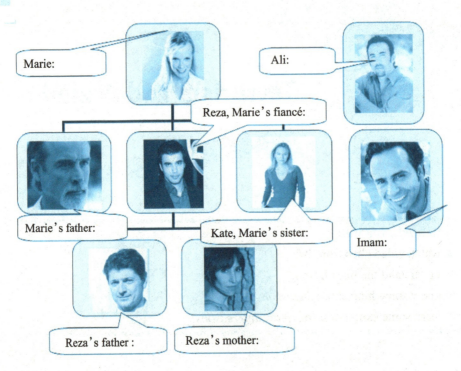

Task 2 This video clip features several characters. What more do you know about them?

Zeza: _____
_____.

Marie: _____
_____.

Section B Story Retelling
Watch the video clip again, then work in pairs and give more details based on the hints below.

1. A nuclear bomb will probably go off today. The U.S. president and officials have a conference.

2. President and Prime Minister of some Middle Eastern state have a conversation on the phone.

3. Reza is under criminal investigation and Marie shoots Reza and the agent.

4. Ali calls Marie and asks her to pick up the trigger.

5. Imam tries to convince Ali of giving up killing innocent people.

6. Marie asks Kate for badge to pass through.

78

Unit 7 Terrorism and Prejudices

Part II Language Appreciation

Section A Language Input

Task 1

Watch the video clip twice and fill in the missing information.

(*door bell*)

Kate: Oh! You're here! Welcome.
Reza's Father: So nice to see you, Kate.
Kate: Come on in.
Reza's Mother: Thank you. The house looks beautiful.
Kate: Oh, thank you. Well... you must be tired. Let's go into the living room.
Reza's Father: OK. So, how is everyone _____ _____?
Kate: Not too bad.
Reza's Mother: Where is Reza?
Kate: Um, well, there's a small problem we're _____ _____.
Reza's Father: What kind of problem?
Kate: Um, some men from the government are here talking to him.
Reza's Father: About?
Kate: It's a criminal investigation.
Reza's Father: Criminal investigation. I don't understand.
Kate: It's very _____.
Reza's Mother: Kate, what is going on?
Kate: It would be best if Reza told you himself.
Reza's Father: Told us what?
Kate: They're talking to Reza about his _____ _____ in terrorist activities.
Reza's Father: That is _____!
Reza's Mother: This must be a mistake.
Kate: That's what they're trying to find out.
Reza's Father: You see? Your country, you talk about _____, you talk about freedom, but you treat every Middle Easterner like he was a terrorist!
Kate: No! No, of course not. I'm sure it'll all get _____ _____.
Bob: Rima, Hassan...
Reza's Father: Bob, do you know about this?
Bob: They just _____ _____ about an hour ago. I know nothing else. I'm sorry. Don't worry. I'm sure it's nothing.

美剧与美国社会文化

Task 2
Watch the video clip, and translate the following Chinese expressions into English.

登录(网络)	
启动(电脑)	
(网络)终端	
(黑客)入侵	
安装程序	
有……权限	

Task 3
Translate the following lines into English, pay special attention to the parts in color, and then watch the video clip and check.

1. 你为什么鬼鬼祟祟的?
   _____?

2. 妈妈去世后,我和爸爸为你付出了一切。
   _____.

3. 你可能被疯子洗脑了吧?
   _____?

Section B Language Output
Watch video clips in this section, and then choose one clip to dub or role play.
Clip1: US. President—Prime Minster of some Middle Eastern state
Clip2: Kate, Bob, Reza's father and mother ...
Clip 3: Marie—Kate

Words and Expressions

Words

triple-sourced	[ˈtriplsɔːst]	adj.	有三个消息来源
credibility	[ˌkrediˈbiləti]	n.	可信性
suspected	[səˈspektid]	adj.	有嫌疑的
fundamentalist	[ˌfʌndəˈmentlist]	n.	原教旨主义者
fatality	[fəˈtæləti]	n.	死亡

Unit 7   Terrorism and Prejudices

surveillance	[sə:'veiləns]	n.	监视,监管
coincidence	[kəu'insidəns]	n.	巧合
extract	[ik'strækt]	v.	取出;摘录
confess	[kən'fes]	v.	承认,坦白
jurisdiction	[ˌdʒuəris'dikʃən]	n.	管辖权,司法权
affiliation	[əˌfili'eiʃən]	n.	联盟;从属关系
tenet	['ti:net]	n.	信条,教义
unimpeded	[ˌʌnim'pi:did]	adj.	未受阻的
level	['levəl]	v.	瞄准
retaliate	[ri'tælieit]	v.	报复
absurd	[əb'sə:d]	adj.	荒谬的
terminal	['tə:minəl]	n.	终端机
trigger	['trigə]	n.	[电子] 触发器
locker	['lɔkə]	n.	有锁的存物柜
combination	[kɔmbi'neiʃən]	n.	(保险锁等的)暗码
imam	[i'mɑ:m]	n.	伊玛目(教长)
accusation	[ækju'zeiʃən]	n.	指控
Koran	[kɔ'rɑ:n]	n.	《可兰经》,《古兰经》
noncombatant	[ˌnɔn'kɔmbətənt]	n.	非战斗人员,平民
twist	[twist]	v.	扭曲
prophet	['prɔfit]	n.	先知
Allah	['ælə]	n.	安拉,真主
aggressor	[ə'gresə]	n.	侵略者
badge	[bædʒ]	n.	徽章;通行证
pathetic	[pə'θetik]	n.	可怜的
hypocrisy	[hi'pɔkrisi]	n.	伪善
ungrateful	[ˌʌn'greitful]	adj.	忘恩负义的
lunatic	['lju:nətik]	n.	疯子

Phrases and Idioms

suicide bomber: 自杀性炸弹

go off: to explode 爆炸

under surveillance: 在监视之下

pick somebody up: (*informal*) to take into custody 关押

— The police picked up 12 suspects in early-morning raids.

— The police picked them up, but the judges just let them go.

splinter group: 分裂出来的小派别

美剧与美国社会文化

loud and clear: if an idea is expressed loud and clear, it is expressed very clearly in a way that is easy to understand 清楚明白的(地)
— Tom: If I've told you once, I've told you a thousand times: Stop it! Do you hear me?
— Bill: Yes, loud and clear. I hear you loud and clear.

sort out: (*fig.*) to study a problem and figure it out 整理;找出解决方法
— Let's sort out this mess and settle it once and for all.

log on: to begin to use a computer system, as by entering a password, etc. 登录(网络)
— I always log on before I get my first cup of coffee.

snoop around: to look around in a place, trying to find out something secret or about someone else's affairs 到处打探
— Why are you snooping around my house?

Proper Names

Defense: 国防部
CIA (Central Intelligence Agency): 中央情报局
FBI (Federal Bureau of Investigation): (美国)联邦调查局

Part III Culture and Society Focus

Section A   Proportion of Different Religions in the United States: What are the major religions in the United States?

Major Religious Traditions in the U.S. (Among All Adults) %							
Christian	Jewish	Buddhist	Muslim	Hindu	Other religions / faiths	unaffiliated	Don't know / Refused
78.4	1.7	0.7	0.6	0.4	1.5	16.1	0.8

Source: "Muslim Americans: Middle Class and Mostly Mainstream," Few Research Center, 2007
Note: Due to rounding, figures may not be added to 100.

Section B   Terrorism

● Why is Reza under criminal investigation?
● Why does Marie betray her own country?

Unit 7   Terrorism and Prejudices

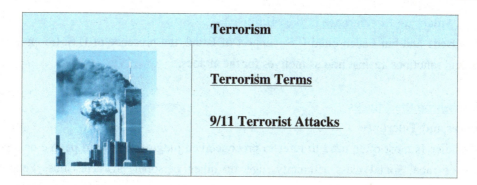

Terrorism
Terrorism Terms
9/11 Terrorist Attacks

Terrorism Terms

Terrorism

People define "terrorism" from different political or religious standpoints so that they do not have a unanimous definition on it. The common definition of "terrorism" only refers to those violent acts which are intended to create fear (terror), are perpetrated for a religious, political or ideological goal; and deliberately target or disregard the safety of non-combatants (civilians).

Religious Terrorism

It is terrorism performed by groups or individuals, the motivation of which is typically rooted in faith-based tenets. Terrorist acts throughout the centuries have been performed on religious grounds with the hope to either spread or enforce a system of belief, viewpoint or opinion. Religious terrorism does not in itself necessarily define a specific religious standpoint or view, but instead usually defines an individual or a group view or interpretation of that belief system's teachings.

9/11 Terrorist Attacks

The September 11 attacks were a series of four coordinated suicide attacks upon the United States in New York City and the Washington, D.C. areas on September 11, 2001. On that Tuesday morning, 19 terrorists from the Islamist militant group Al-Qaeda (in English, it means the base) hijacked four passenger jets. The hijackers intentionally crashed two planes into the Twin Towers of the World Trade Center in New York City; both towers collapsed within two hours. Hijackers crashed the third jet into the Pentagon in Arlington, Virginia. The fourth jet, crashed into a field near Shanksville, Pennsylvania after passengers attempted to take control before it could reach the hijackers' intended target in Washington, D.C. Nearly 3,000 people died in the attacks. Suspicion quickly fell on al-Qaeda, and in 2004, the group's leader Osama bin Laden, who had initially denied involvement, claimed responsibility for the attacks. In May 2011, after years at large, bin Laden was found and killed by the U.S. government.

Motives: American Interference in the Middle East

Al-Qaeda and bin Laden cited U.S. support of Israel, the presence of U.S. troops in Saudi Arabia, and sanctions against Iraq as motives for the attacks.

Reasons behind the Attacks
Prejudices and Tolerance

Prejudice is most often used to refer to preconceived judgments toward people or a person because of race, social class, ethnicity, age or other personal characteristics. People are socialized to have prejudices in the sense that they are influenced by families, schools, mass media from different social, economic and cultural backgrounds. So, when differences arise, prejudices often occur. It is a question how people face differences and prejudices: to tolerate or to have conflicts.

Reconstruction of the World

Al-Qaeda leaders and supporters argue that over the last millennium the West has expelled Islamic group from the Middle East (for example, Israel), Europe(for example, Balkans) to North Africa. They assert that Islamic group has a legitimate claim on the above areas. They want to reconstruct the world and expand the global influence of Islam.

The US after 9/11

The United States responded to the attacks by launching the War on Terror and invading Afghanistan to depose the Taliban, which had harbored al-Qaeda. Many countries strengthened their anti-terrorism legislation and expanded law enforcement powers.

Numerous incidents of harassment and hate crimes against Muslims and South Asians were reported in the days following the 9/11 attacks.

According to an academic study, people perceived to be Middle Easterner were as likely to be victims of hate crimes as followers of Islam during this time. The study also found a similar increase in hate crimes against people who may have been perceived as Muslims, Arabs and

Unit 7 Terrorism and Prejudices

others thought to be of Middle Eastern origin. Various crimes such as vandalism, arson, assault, shootings, harassment, and threats in numerous places were documented.

Task 1   Warm up

Personal Awareness Survey

Attitude Towards Others — Use this personal awareness survey to evaluate your attitude towards people who differ from you and situations that differ from yours. (Source: The Spokane Task Force on Race Relations)

1. **List any thoughts and feelings you have when you are exposed to people different from yourself and situations that are unfamiliar. Circle the feelings that are strongest.**

2. **When you were growing up, what were your parents' attitudes toward other racial groups, people with disabilities, people with different socio-economic backgrounds, expectation of sex roles, gay, lesbian, transgender, and bisexuals?**
   (a) open and friendly
   (b) indifferent
   (c) prejudiced and unfriendly
   Is your attitude toward these diverse groups of people different from that of your parents? If yes, explain how:

3. **How does your attitude toward others compare with the views held by your friends?**
   (a) same
   (b) slightly different
   (c) different
   (d) very different

4. **Which one of the following items do you feel now has the greatest influence on your attitude?**
   (a) your upbringing
   (b) personal philosophy or religious ideology
   (c) news media, commentators, writers, or special friends

Task 2　Presentation

If you have some conflicts with people who are different from yourself and are from other social, economic and cultural backgrounds, how do you deal with the conflicts? Tell a story with the topic of "my experience to deal with conflicts."

Step 1　Prepare

Who is he/she? (Who are they?)

In what way are you different from each other?

How do you deal with differences?

Step 2　Your Draft

Useful Expressions
open mindedness
tolerant
realizing and understanding differences

Useful Sentence Patterns
it happened on a windy morning ...
then, ...
eventually ...
the lesson I have learned is that ...

Step 3　Rehearse

Practice your presentation with a classmate.

Listener task: Identify the following elements for narrative: when, where, why, what and how.

Step 4　Present

Present it to the whole class.

Listener task: Listen carefully on how the presenter deals with the differences. What would you do if you were him/her?

Unit 7 Terrorism and Prejudices

Part IV Writing

Write about the following topic: Will one culture probably assimilate another culture?

Some culture is more pervasive, like American culture. Do you think it will probably assimilate another culture? Give your reasons and relevant examples.

Write an essay of at least 200 words.

Functional Sentence Patterns

Analyzing Reasons:
- The underlying reasons for it might be ...
- There are numerous reasons why..., and I would explore only a few of the most important ones here.
- A number of factors are accountable for this situation.
- The factors that contribute to this situation include ...
- One of the basic/primary factor is that ...

Additional Information

24: It is an American television series produced for the Fox Network and syndicated worldwide, starring Kiefer Sutherland as Counter Terrorist Unit (CTU) agent Jack Bauer. Each 24-episode season covers 24 hours in the life of Bauer, using the real time method of narration.

Plot: Bauer is the only character to have appeared in every episode of the series. The series begins with his working for the Los Angeles-based Counter Terrorist Unit (CTU), in which he is a highly-proficient agent with an "ends justify the means" approach, regardless of the perceived morality of some of his actions. Throughout the series most of the main plot elements unfold like a political thriller. A typical plot has Bauer racing against the clock as he attempts to thwart multiple terrorist plots, including presidential assassination attempts, nuclear, biological and chemical threats, cyber attacks, as well as conspiracies which deal with government and corporate corruption.

Critique and achievements: Although critically acclaimed, the series has been criticized for its depictions of torture as effective and its negative depictions of Muslims. Nevertheless, the show won numerous awards over its eight seasons, including Best Drama Series at the 2003 Golden Globe Awards and Outstanding Drama Series at the 2006 Primetime Emmy Awards. At the conclusion of its eighth and final season, *24* became the longest-running espionage-themed television drama ever, surpassing both *Mission: Impossible* and *The Avengers*.

> *Fact File*
> Kiefer Sutherland (1966—): actor, producer, director (starring Jack Bauer)
> - Golden Globe Award for Best Actor — Television Series Drama (2002)
> - Primetime Emmy Award for Outstanding Lead Actor in a Drama Series (2006)
> - Primetime Emmy Award for Outstanding Drama Series (2006)
> - Satellite Award for Best Actor — Television Series Drama (2002—2003)
> - Screen Actors Guild Award for Outstanding Performance by a Male Actor in a Drama Series (2004, 2006)

Unit 8

Gender and Work

In this unit, you will:
- watch video clips from *Desperate Housewives*;
- understand the lines from it;
- know something about *women at work*;
- learn some expressions on *describing data*.

Part I Story Exploration

Section A Character Introduction

Task 1 Watch the video clip once and write down the identities of the characters in the graph.

Background: *The characters in the pictures below are at Weisman Leadership Conference.*

| president of Amtech | plus one | CFO of Morris Technologies |
| lawyer | plus one | |

美剧与美国社会文化

Task 2 This video clip features several characters. What more do you know about them?

Lynette & Tom: _____

Lee & Bob: _____

Meg Butler: _____

Section B Story Retelling

Watch the video clip again, put the sentences below in the right order and then retell the story.

1 While Meg Butler is having a spa, Lynette steals her lanyard(胸牌) and goes to the seminar. Then she is mistaken for Meg to give a keynote speech.

2 Lynette has a small talk with Meg Butler. She is informed that she won't be seeing Chris Cavanaugh at the seminar.

3 Lynette is not interested in Japanese flower arranging(日式插花).

4 Meg comes back furiously to the seminar to get her lanyard back.

5 Lynette is tired of doing the housework. At that moment, she is excited to be invited to the Weisman Leadership Conference.

Sequence: ○ ⇨ ○ ⇨ ○ ⇨ ○ ⇨ ○

Unit 8　Gender and Work

Section A　Language Input

Task 1　Translate the following sentences into English, pay special attention to the parts in color, and then watch the video clip and check.

1. 你启动洗碗机了吗?
   _____?

2. 我们也没有牛奶了。
   _____.

3. 我的子宫不好用了,但我的听力还好。(子宫：uterus)
   _____.

4. 整个地方真是乱七八糟。
   _____.

5. 我正式宣布我太累了,照顾不了你们了。
   _____.

Task 2　Watch the video clip, and translate the English expressions into Chinese.

a-list	
show somebody the rope	
bone-crushing handshake	
work one's way up the corporate ladder	

Task 3　Watch the video clip twice and fill in the missing information.

Unknown Lady A: Ikebana is all about bringing together nature and humanity. The three main branches or sushi, represent chi—earth, Ten—heaven, and jin—man.

Lynette:　　Interesting. _____ _____ _____ _____. How about this insignificant clump of moss? We could stuff it down at the bottom where it will only speak when spoken to.

Lee:　　Does my chi look a little droopy?

Lynette:　　Did you hear me?

Lee:　　Yes. Yes. Lynette, I heard you. I heard you during yoga, during the _____ _____. All through Salsa dancing. Life is unfair. Ale!

Lynette:　　I'm sorry. But I came here to _____ _____ _____ and _____ _____, not to pretend that putting sticks in a vase is art.

Unknown Lady B: Are we still having a problem?

91

美剧与美国社会文化

Lynette: Yes, we still are. Doesn't it _____ _____ all _____ that we're stuck in our gilded cage, forbidden to go to interesting seminars just because _____ _____ ?

Unknown Lady C: No. This is fun. I really feel like I'm in Japan.

Lynette: This is the United States of America in the 21st century. Not some oppressive patriarchal regime. It may be small and red, but this lanyard is no better than a burka.

Unknown Lady B: Oh, dear!

Lynette: We need to _____ _____ _____ and demand to be let inside!

Lee: If you are not gonna use the rest of your flowers, can I ...

Lynette: Come on! _____ _____ ! If we do it together, we will not be denied!

Unknown Lady B: 4:00, people. I think you've all earned a cocktail.

Lynette: No! No! No! Do not drink those. Those are the ... the cocktail of oppression made from equal parts of tyranny and blind obedience, and ... oh, screw it.

Section B   Language Output

Watch video clips in this section, and then choose one clip to dub or role play.

Clip 1: Lynette—her family

Clip 2: Lynette—Meg Butler ...

Unit 8　Gender and Work

Words and Expressions

Words

dishwasher	[ˈdɪʃˌwɒʃə]	n.	洗碗机
uterus	[ˈjuːtərəs]	n.	子宫
spot	[spɒt]	v.	认出，看见
a-list		adj.	重要的，一流的
		n.	要员名单
fancy	[ˈfænsi]	adj.	引人注目的
hotshot	[ˈhɒtʃɒt]	n.	专家，牛人
council	[ˈkaunsəl]	n.	委员会
seminar	[ˈseminɑː]	n.	研讨会
participant	[pɑːˈtisipənt]	n.	参与者
corporate	[ˈkɔːpərit]	adj.	公司的
buddy	[ˈbʌdi]	n.	伙伴，兄弟
scavenger hunt	[ˈskævindʒə hʌnt]		寻物游戏（一种找寻事先藏好物品的游戏）
clump	[klʌmp]	n.	块，丛
droopy	[ˈdruːpi]	adj.	下垂的
gilded	[ˈgildid]	adj.	镀金的
oppressive	[əˈpresiv]	adj.	压迫的
patriarchal	[ˌpeitriˈɑːkəl]	adj.	由族长统治的
regime	[reiˈʒiːm]	n.	政体
lanyard	[ˈlænjəd]	n.	胸前挂的吊牌
burka	[ˈbəːkə]	n.	（蒙住全身，只露出眼睛的）长袍
tyranny	[ˈtirəni]	n.	暴政，专政
obedience	[əˈbiːdjəns]	n.	顺从
spouse	[spauz]	n.	配偶
shove	[ʃʌv]	v.	胡乱塞进
nutmeg	[ˈnʌtmeg]	n.	肉豆蔻
rascal	[ˈræskəl]	n.	坏蛋，淘气鬼
ale	[ɑːˈle]		（西班牙语）加油

Phrases and Idioms

show sb. the rope: to explain to someone how to do a job or activity 告诉某人怎样做
　　— The new secretary started today so I spent most of the morning showing her the ropes.

pull some strings: to use influence (with someone to get something done) 走后门

— I can get it done easily by pulling a few strings.

— Is it possible to get anything done around here without pulling some strings?

plus one: When one is invited to a party or meeting with his/her spouse/date, then this spouse/date is called a plus one. 在此视频中意为家属。

Part III Culture and Society Focus

Section A Forbes

Forbes is an American publishing and media company. Its flagship publication, the *Forbes* magazine, is published biweekly. Its primary competitors in the national business magazine category are *Fortune*, which is also published biweekly, in addtion to *Business Week*. The magazine is well-known for its lists, including its lists of the richest Americans (the Forbes 400) and its list of billionaires. The motto of *Forbes* magazine is "The Capitalist Tool."

Section B Women & Work

- Why won't Lynette be seeing Chris Cavanaugh at the seminar?
- What do you think of Meg's remark "some of us spent our lives working our way up the corporate ladder, and others just married who did"?

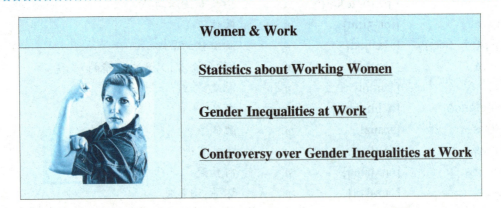

Statistics about Working Women
In the USA:

According to the 2010 publication of the United States Labor Department,

- Of the 123 million women aged 16 years and over in the U.S., 72 million, or 58.6 percent, were labor force participants—working or looking for work.

Unit 8 Gender and Work

- Women comprised 47 percent of the total U.S. labor force.

In China:

In 2008, 67.5 percent of Chinese women over 16 were employed, according to Yang Juhua working in the Population and Development Studies Center of Renmin University of China, citing World Bank statistics. That was a drop from the most recent Chinese government data, from 2000, showing that 71.52 percent of women from 16 through 54 were employed, compared with 82.47 percent of men from 16 through 59. Ms. Yang has calculated that women earn 63.5 percent of men's salaries, a drop from 64.8 in 2000.

[Source: Didi Kirsten Tatlow, *New York Times*, November 25, 2010]

Gender Inequalities at Work

Gender Differences

Gender differences not only result from natural biology, such as hormones, chromosomes, brain size and genetics, but also from cultural influence. As Anthony Giddens in his *Sociology* said, "Gender differences are not biologically determined, they are culturally produced."

Socialization & Gender Socialization

Socialization is the means by which human infants begin to acquire the skills necessary to perform as a functioning member of their society. It is the most influential learning process one can experience.

An important part of socialization is the learning of culturally defined gender roles. "Gender socialization" refers to the learning of behaviors and attitudes considered appropriate for a given sex. Boys learn to be boys and girls learn to be girls. The learning of gender roles is helped by social agencies such as the family, school, friends, and the media.

For example, when they are children, boys and girls are given different toys, dressed in different colors, and even read different picture books and watch different TV programs. Boys are expected to be "brave," "decisive" and "future bread-winner" while girls to be "gentle," "careful," and "future home-keeper."

Gender and Inequalities

Men and women are socialized into different roles. That results in gender inequalities which are reflected in the following aspects.

※ **Labor Force Participation**

Figure 1 shows U.S. labor force participation of men and women from 1970 to 2007. Who participate more in labor force? How does women's participation change over the years?

Figure 1 U.S. Labor Force Participation of Men and Women, 1970 to 2007

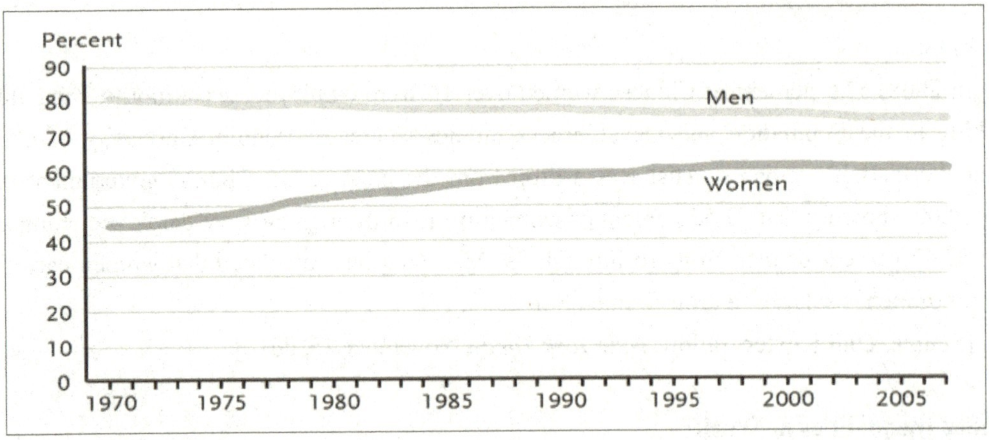

〔Source: Estimates and projection from the US Census Bureau, Bureau of Statistics and Pew Hispanic Centre〕

※ **Occupational Structure and Earnings**

Figure 2 shows that some highly sex-typed jobs have changed little from 1970 to 2007 in the U.S.

Figure 2 Examples of Highly Sex-typed Jobs that Have Changed Little

	Percent of people in occupation who are women				
	1970	1980	1990	2000	2007
Secretaries	98.1	98.8	98.6	96.5	96.1
Registered nurses	97.8	96.2	94.7	92.8	91.2
Dental assistants	98.6	97.9	97.1	96.8	97.1
Kindergarten and earlier school teachers	98.3	96.7	98.1	98.1	97.2
Carpenters	1.6	1.9	1.9	2.0	1.9
Airplane pilots and navigators	1.6	1.6	3.8	4.2	4.9
Automobile mechanics	1.6	1.4	2.1	2.1	1.7

〔Source: IPUMS Census samples, 1850—2007 (variable: occ1990)〕

Figure 3 shows the U.S. women's and men's weekly earning for full time by age in the fourth quarter of 2010.

Unit 8   Gender and Work

Figure 3   Women's and Men's Weekly Earnings for Full Time Work by Age in Fourth Quarter 2010

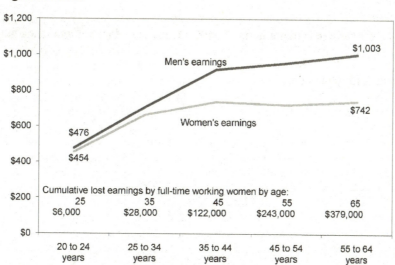

(Source: Department of Labor, Chief Economist's Office, using Current Population Survey Data)

Controversy over Gender Inequalities at Work

Some people insist that gender discrimination is a key cause of women's lower pay and lower positions at work.

- Although discrimination against women in the labor market has declined, some discrimination still continue to exist.
- Women's caring responsibilities for the child(ren) and family tends to be undervalued.

Other people argued that the difference in salaries between male and female workers came down to "individual lifestyle preferences". That is to say, the choice of millions of mothers to put children and family before careers is the chief reason given for the disparity between men and women that emerged after 30.

Task 1   Brainstorm: Why are they tired?

美剧与美国社会文化

Task 2 Debate

Step 1 Choose your side and prepare.

Pro: The place for women is in her home.   **vs.**   **Con:** The place for women is in her work.

List your arguments for your side.

Step 2 Debate

List the arguments of the opposite group and your refuting arguments.

The Opposite Group's Arguments	Your Own Arguments

Step 3 Present

Report your group's arguments to the whole class.

Listener task: Which group's arguments are more convincing? Give the reasons to support yourself.

Part IV Writing

Write about the following topic:

The graph below shows the proportion of U.S. Women in Business in 2011.

Unit 8 Gender and Work

Summarize the information by selecting and reporting the main features, find out what phenomenon the graph shows and explain it.

Write at least 200 words.

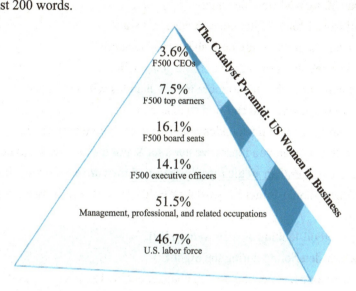

[**Source:**

Catalyst Research

Catalyst, 2011 Catalyst Census: Fortune 500 Women Board Directors (2011).

Catalyst, 2011 Catalyst Census: Fortune 500 Women Executive Officers and Top Earners (2011).

Bureau of Labor Statistics, 2010 Current Population Suurvey, "Employed persons by detailed occupation, sex race, and Hispanic or Latino ethnicity."

Bureau of Labor Statistics, 2010 Current Population Suurvey, "Employment status of the civilian noninstitutional population by age, sex, and race."]

Functional Sentence Patterns

Describing Data
- According to /As is shown in the table / figure / chart ...
- Among the most striking trends in the charts are the fact that ...
- It has increased ... compared with that of ...
- It can be seen from the chart /diagram /table /graph /figures /statistics that ...
- From the table / data / results / information above, it can /may be seen/ concluded / shown /estimated /calculated /inferred that ...

美剧与美国社会文化

Fun Time

10 Differences between Men and Women

- A man will pay $2 for a $1 item he wants.
  A woman will pay $1 for a $2 item that she doesn't want.
- A woman worries about the future until she gets a husband.
  A man never worries about the future until he gets a wife.
- A successful man is one who makes more money than his wife can spend.
  A successful woman is one who can find such a man.
- To be happy with a man you must understand him a lot & love him a little.
  To be happy with a woman you must love her a lot & not try to understand her at all.
- Married men live longer than single men, but married men are a lot more willing to die.
- Any married man should forget his mistakes — there's no use in two people remembering the same thing.
- Men wake up as good-looking as they went to bed.
  Women somehow deteriorate during the night.
- A woman marries a man expecting he will change, but he doesn't.
  A man marries a woman expecting that she won't change, and she does.
- A woman has the last word in any argument.
  Anything a man says after that is the beginning of a new argument.
- There are 2 times when a man doesn't understand a woman — before marriage & after marriage.

Unit 9

Gun Violence

> **In this unit, you will:**
> - watch video clips from *Grey's Anatomy*;
> - understand the lines from it;
> - know something about *gun culture in USA*;
> - learn some expressions on *giving examples*.

Part 1 Story Exploration

Section A Character Introduction

Background: Mrs. Clark has a severe brain damage, and can't sustain her life without a respirator's support. As she signed an advanced directive 3 years ago which specifically requested no mechanical ventilation, and there is nothing that can be done to save her life, her doctor-in-charge, Dr. Webber, decides to give up. However, Mr. Clark goes to talk with the Chief, Dr. Shepherd, hoping not to unplug the machine.

Characters that will appear in this video clip:

  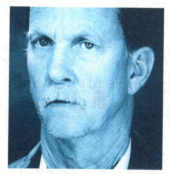

Dr. Derek Shepherd (the Chief)　　Dr. Richard Webber　　Mr. Clark

美剧与美国社会文化

Lexie Grey

April

Reed

Watch the video clip, and exchange what you know about Mr. Clark with your neighbor.

_____

_____

Section B Story Retelling

Watch the video clip again, then work in pairs and retell the story with the help of the following questions.

1. Why does Dr. Shepherd insist on Dr. Webber's decision?	2. Is Mr. Clark willing to accept Dr. Shepherd's decision?	3. When Mr. Clark appears again in the hospital, what is he doing in the hospital?
Tips: advanced directive around-the-clock care	Tips: wake up, unplug respirator	Tips: look for
4. Why does Mr. Clark kill Reed?	5. Why does Mr. Clark want to kill Dr. Shepherd?	6. What does Dr. Shepherd say to Mr. Clark that almost makes him give up killing him?
Tips: tour guide, surgeon, irritate	Tips: be God	Tips: make mistakes
7. Where does Mr. Clark get his gun and ammunition? Will he kill Dr. Webber?		
Tips: on sale		

Unit 9 Gun Violence

Part II Language Appreciation

Section A Language Input

Task 1 Watch the video clip twice and fill in the missing words.

Dr. Shepherd: Mr. Clark, I'm deeply sorry for your ...for your _____.

Mr. Clark: No, no no no, don't speak about my wife _____ _____ she's dead. She's still here. She could wake up.

Dr. Shepherd: She's not gonna wake up, Mr. Clark, not with the _____ _____ she suffered.

Mr. Clark: You don't know that.

Dr. Webber: Mr. Clark, if we don't _____ your wife's directive, if we ignore her wishes...

Mr. Clark: She _____ that form three years ago...

Dr. Shepherd: Her health will deteriorate. She'll lose body mass. She'll have no _____ _____.

Dr. Webber: She'll require _____ care, and that can become very expensive very quickly.

Mr. Clark: I don't care about that.

Dr. Shepherd: It'll be _____ _____ for either of you. And that's why your wife signed the advanced directive. She didn't want to _____ _____ live her life this way. And she didn't want you to live your life this way either.

Mr. Clark: Don't you speak for my wife. Don't you _____ speak for my wife.

Dr. Shepherd: I'm sorry, Mr. Clark, but the ethics committee has reviewed your case. We are _____ _____ law to obey her wishes.

Mr. Clark: If you _____ my wife...you'll be killing her.

Dr. Shepherd: I'm sorry. You should uh... _____ _____ _____ _____ you need to call your family...to say good-bye.

Mr. Clark: There's no one to call. We didn't _____ _____ _____. It was just us. We didn't have any _____. It's just me.

Task 2 Translate the following lines into English, pay special attention to the parts in color, and then watch the video clip and check.

1. 必须得有人保护人们避免受你的伤害。

   _____.

2. 我当医生并不是因为我想成为上帝。我成为医生是因为我想要拯救生命。

   _____.

3. 我是人, 我也犯错, 我也有缺点, 我们都是这样的。

   _____.

美剧与美国社会文化

Task 3 Some lines by Dr. Webber in this episode are considered classic by netizens. Can you fill in the missing words and translate the part in bold into Chinese?

Mr. Clark:　　Hey.

Dr. Webber:　What's it gonna be, Mr. Clark? Me or you? You shoot me, S.W.A.T.'s gonna get you. And they're not gonna shoot you. They're gonna capture you and they're gonna take you to prison. Or you shoot yourself ... then you're free ... _____ ... Maybe get to see your wife again. So you have a _____ _____ _____. Me or you? A life in prison ... or an _____ with your wife?

Mr. Clark:　　S..._____ _____.

Dr. Webber:　**See, I've _____ . I've really really _____ . I've _____ . I've been devastated. I've been _____ . I've gone to _____ _____ _____ . And I've also known _____ . And _____ . And I've had a great love. See ... death for me is not _____ . It's an ... _____ of a _____ _____ . And I'm not afraid to die. The question is, are you? A life in prison or an ... with your wife. Me or you? Your choice.**

Section B　Language Output

Watch video clips in this section, and then choose one clip to dub or role play.

Clip 1: Dr. Shepherd—Dr. Webber—Mr. Clark

Clip 2: Mr. Clark—Dr. Shepherd

Clip 3: Mr. Clark—Dr. Webber

Words and Expressions

Words

deteriorate	[dɪˈtɪərɪəreɪt]	v.	恶化,变质,衰退
around-the-clock			连续不断的,昼夜不停的 =round-the-clock
unplug	[ˌʌnˈplʌg]	v.	拔开
respirator	[ˈrespəreɪtə]	n.	呼吸器
seizure	[ˈsiːʒə]	n.	(疾病)突然发作
dude	[djuːd]	n.	〈口〉哥们;花花公子
flawed	[flɔːd]	adj.	有瑕疵的,有缺陷的
devastate	[ˈdevəsteɪt]	vt.	毁坏
aisle	[aɪl]	n.	侧廊,通道
ammunition	[ˌæmjuˈnɪʃən]	n.	军火,弹药

Unit 9 Gun Violence

ammo	[ˈæməu]	n.	弹药 =ammunition
flask	[flæsk]	n.	细颈瓶,烧瓶
afterlife	[ˈɑːftəlaif]	n.	来生,死后(灵魂)的生活

Phrases and Idioms

screw you：(*slang*) 去你的

immune system：免疫系统

advanced directive：Generally, an Advanced Directive is a written document which tells people how to make your medical decisions which you can't make for yourself. 事先说明

the ethics committee：伦理委员会

see...through: to continue to work at (something) until it is completed 把……做完
— Yes. It was our last case together and I wanted to see it through to the end.

hand down: 宣布
— The city council will hand down the budget on Monday.

a hell of: 用来加重语气
— The result is a hell of a wonderful show where applause don't stop.

pack ... into: 装进
— You can easily roll up the feather-light sheets and pack into your bag.

Proper Names

Vodka [ˈvɔdkə] *n.* 伏特加酒

S.W.A.T.: A S.W.A.T. means special weapons and tactics team. Its duties include: performing hostage rescues and counter-terrorism operations; serving high risk arrest and search warrants; subduing barricaded suspects; and engaging heavily-armed criminals. 警察队伍中的一支特种作战单位

Part III Culture and Society Focus

Background information about the video:
Finally, 11 people were killed by Mr. Clark and even more injured.
- Watch the video clip, where does Mr. Clark buy his gun and ammunition?
- If Mr. Clark can't get a gun, and performs his revenge in whatever other ways, can the result be as horrifying as in the video?

Gun Culture	
	Gun Laws **Origin** **Present-day Gun Culture in the USA**

Gun Laws

China

According to the PRC law, there are firearms regulations and according to those regulations "whoever, in violation of firearm-control regulations, secretly keeps firearms or ammunition and refuses to relinquish them shall be sentenced to fixed-term imprisonment of not more than two years or criminal detention."

USA

Gun laws in the United States regulate the sale, possession, and use of firearms and ammunition. In the USA, the protection against infringement of the right to keep and bear arms is addressed in the Second Amendment to the United States Constitution.

In 2008, the Supreme Court ruled that the Second Amendment protects an individual's right to own a gun for personal use, unconnected with service in a militia. It also specifically stated that individuals have the right to keep a loaded gun at home for self-defense.

However, state laws vary, and are independent of existing federal firearms laws, although they are sometimes broader or more limited in scope than the federal laws.

Unit 9 Gun Violence

Table 1 Gun Laws in New York & California

Subject/Law	Long guns		Handguns	
	New York	California	New York	California
State permit to purchase?	No	No	Yes	No
Firearm registration?	Yes	Yes	Yes	Yes
"Assault weapon" law	Yes	Yes	Yes	Yes
Owner license required?	Varies	No	Yes	No
Carry permits issued?	Yes	N/A	Yes	Partial

Origin

Firearms became readily identifiable symbols of the westward expansion.

In 1970, the noted historian Richard Hofstadter used the phrase "gun culture" to describe America's long-held affection for guns.

The American gun culture is founded on three factors: the proliferation of firearms since the earliest days of the nation, the connection between personal ownership of weapons and the country's revolutionary and frontier history, and the cultural mythology regarding the gun in the frontier and in modern life.

Present-day Gun Culture in the USA

Types of firearms

Firearms have been viewed in only three general classes by gun control advocates.

Table 2

Types of firearms	Pictures	Uses
Long gun (rifles and shotguns)		Sporting, hunting

107

(continuing)

Handgun		self-defense
Automatic and semi-automatic weapon		Military use

Gun owning facts in the USA

Based upon surveys, the following are estimates of private firearm ownership in the U.S. as of 2010:

	Households with a Gun	Adults Owning a Gun	Adults Owning a Handgun
Percentage	40—45%	30—34%	17—19%
Number	47—53 million	70—80 million	40—45 million

Number of guns per capita by country

This is a list of countries by gun ownership rate (number of privately-owned small firearms divided by number of residents).

Table 3

Country	Guns per 100 residents (2007)	Rank (2007)
United States	88.8	1
England and Wales	6.2	88

Anti-gun Culture vs. Pro-gun Culture

There has been a debate about whether guns should be prohibited in the USA. People generally are divided into two sides: anti-gun and pro-gun groups.

※ **Anti-gun Culture**

In recent years, news like the following one is not rare.

News report:
CNN, February 29, 2012

Unit 9 Gun Violence

A third student has died from the shooting rampage at Chardon High School in the US state of Ohio, CNN reported Tuesday.

The suspect allegedly brought a handgun into the school cafeteria, and started shooting just after 7:30 a.m. Monday. Five students were shot at three locations.

The deadliest high school shooting in US history occurred in 1999 at Columbine High School in Colorado, where two senior students killed 12 students and one teacher. The pair then committed suicide.

Researches:

A number of surveys have found that a gun kept at home is far more likely to be used in violence, an accident, or a suicide attempt than self defense. Researcher David Hemenway who works at the Harvard School of Public Health concluded that people do stupid things when angry or depressed, and the presence of a gun helps make that stupidity fatal.

Gun Crime Facts:

In the United States, firearms remain the most common method of suicide, accounting for 52.1% of all suicides committed during 2005.

What can you read from the following two tables?

Table 4 Intentional homicides (谋杀) by country/region

Country/Region	% homicides with firearms	Firearm homicide rate per 100,000 pop.	Non-firearm homicide rate per 100,000 pop.	Overall homicide rate per 100,000 pop.	Citizens may own guns
England & Wales	8	0.12	1.33	1.45	No
Hong Kong, China	2	0.01	0.55	0.56	No
United States	65	2.97	1.58	4.55	Yes

〔Source: United Nations Office on Drugs and Crime, 2000〕

Table 5 Gun crime statistics by US state: 2010

State	Total murders	Total firearms 2010	Handguns murders	Firearms % of all murders	Firearms murders per 100,000 pop.	Firearms robberies per 100,000 pop.	Firearms assaults per 100,000 pop.
UNITED STATES	12,996	8,775	6,009	67.52	2.84	41.67	44.78

〔Source: FBI〕

Costs of gun violence

Gun violence leads to significant monetary costs. It is estimated that gun violence costs the USA $100 billion annually. The two main contributors to the monetary costs are emergency medical care and psychological costs.

※ Pro-gun Culture

News report:

Carolyn Presutti: 19 April 2010, VOA

Some came to the Washington D.C. area Monday to take out their guns in a show of support for gun rights. Others came for a rally in the shadow of the Washington monument "to support the right to keep and bear arms" and to protect the Second Amendment.

Rob Weaver says he would die to protect the Second Amendment if it is threatened.

Gun law advocates say they support the Second Amendment.

"What we are trying to do is make sure the wrong people don't get their hands on guns," said Chad Ramsey. "We think that you ought to have a background check at gun shows. We think you ought to have a background check so that people who are dangerously mentally ill aren't getting their hands on guns."

※ Opinions from netizens:

- I have been shot at (many years ago) but I really don't feel the need to carry a gun. I have no real problem with people that do carry...as long as they are responsible with it.
- Anyone who breaks into my home is going to be on the receiving end of a 12 gauge shotgun loaded with five 3'00 magnum rounds. I live in an area rife with drug dealers and narcotics, and they know not to mess with me because the worst nightmare of a hardened criminal is an armed victim.
- We can get rid of all the guns in this country so only the criminals and military has them.
- Guns will NEVER be taken away from the public, it is the right of the people to possess firearms for their protection.
- Last week I witnessed a man assaulting a woman. Had I been armed, it would have been much easier; I could have merely pointed the gun at him and held him for police. And stories like that happen all the time.

Task 1   Warm up

Watch the following 2 video clips, and find out the uses of a handgun to Bree.

Background of video 1:

Bree is a widow, and her children moved out after getting married, so she lives alone in a house.

Use: _____

Unit 9 Gun Violence

Background of video 2:

The lady who appears in this video is Bree's former neighbor and friend who committed suicide with a handgun in the first episode of the first season in Desperate Wives.

Use: _____

Task 2 Discussion

After reading the materials about gun culture in the USA, you might have your own idea about the benefits and harms of owning a gun. Assuming that owning a gun is legal in China, discuss the following topic with your partners, "Does gun ownership cause or prevent crime?"

Step 1 Survey

Answer the questions in the following questionnaire and compare yours with your partners'.

Question 1	Did you have a toy gun when you were young?	
Question 2	Are you interested in guns? What gun types do you know?	
Question 3	Have you ever experienced shooting a gun? If yes, use an adjective to describe your feeling when or after shooting.	
Question 4	Have you or your family ever been threatened or attacked, such as robbing, breaking-in, etc? Do you think a gun might help at that time?	
Question 5	If permitted legally, do you intend to own a gun?	

Step 2 Prepare

My opinion on "Does gun ownership cause or prevent crime?"

Supporting arguments.

Argument 1:

美剧与美国社会文化

Argument 2:

...

Step 3　Group discussion

Share your opinion and arguments with your partners, and take down others' opinions and arguments.

Step 4　Present

Present your opinion and arguments to the whole class.

Listener task: Take down arguments that might be helpful with your following writing.

Useful Expressions	Your Own Word Box
...pose no real threat to anyone other than their closest friends and family stay away from ... **Functional Sentence Patterns** I've come to the conclusion that ... ... is nothing more than ... **Tip:** More useful expressions about gun control can be found in the above background materials.	

Unit 9　Gun Violence

Part IV　Writing

Based on the above discussion, write about "Does gun ownership cause or prevent crime?"

Give your own opinion, supporting arguments and include any relevant examples from your knowledge or experience. Write at least 200 words.

Functional Sentence Patterns

Giving examples
- A case in point is ...
- Take ... for example
- In my case, ...
- In some cases, ...
- Suppose / Assume / Imagine that ...
- There are many cases in which ...

Additional Information

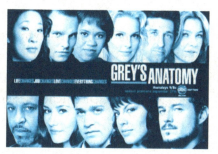

Grey's Anatomy is an American medical drama television series created by Shonda Rhimes. The series premiered on March 27, 2005 on ABC; since then, eight seasons have aired.

Plot: The series follows the lives of interns, residents and their mentors in the fictional Seattle Grace Mercy West Hospital in Seattle, Washington, as they struggle to complete their medical training and maintain personal lives.

Meredith Grey is on the job at Seattle Grace as a first year intern with at least 20 others. Each year the interns are split into groups which are assigned to residents. In Meredith's group are 4 other first-year interns: Cristina Yang, Isobel "Izzie" Stevens, George O'Malley and Alex Karev. Yesterday they were students but today they are doctors at Seattle Grace Hospital. They are participating in the toughest surgical residency program west of Harvard. But their new jobs aren't the only things they have to keep them busy. There are always their personal lives...

Achievements: The show has attained commercial success and critical acclaim. The series, especially during the second and third season, has received a number of awards, among which are the Golden Globe Award for Best Television Series—Drama in 2006, two Emmy nominations for Outstanding Drama Series in 2006 and 2007, and numerous other awards and nominations for acting, writing and directing. So far, the show has received three Emmy awards. In 2010, *Grey's Anatomy* was the fourth-highest revenue earning show for 2010, with US$2.67 million per half hour behind *Desperate Housewives*, *Two and a Half Men* and *American Idol*.

Actors for Dr. Derek Shepherd and Dr. Richard Webber

Dr. Derek Shepherd is portrayed by Patrick Dempsey who has received significant public attention for this role. Dempsey was nominated for Best Performance by an Actor in a Television Series — Drama at the 2006 Golden Globes for the role.

Dr. Richard Webber is portrayed by James Pickens, Jr. (born October 26, 1954). He is best known for this role, and for his supporting role as Deputy Director Alvin Kersh on later seasons of the Fox Network science fiction series *The X-Files*.

Unit 10

Crime Correction

> In this unit, you will:
> - watch video clips from *Prison Break* and *Desperate Housewives*;
> - understand the lines from it;
> - know something about *Crime in the United States*;
> - learn some expressions on *offering measures*.

Part I Story Exploration

Video 1

Section A Character Introduction

Background: Lincoln, L.J.'s father, is accused of murdering Terrence Steadman, the brother of Vice President of the United States Caroline Reynolds. Lincoln is sentenced to death and is incarcerated while he awaits his execution.

What do you know about the following characters in video clip 1 from *Prison Break*? Watch the video clip now and briefly introduce them.

Lisa
L.J.'s mother
Lincoln's ex-girlfriend
Goes to visit L.J.'s father in prison with L.J.

115

美剧与美国社会文化

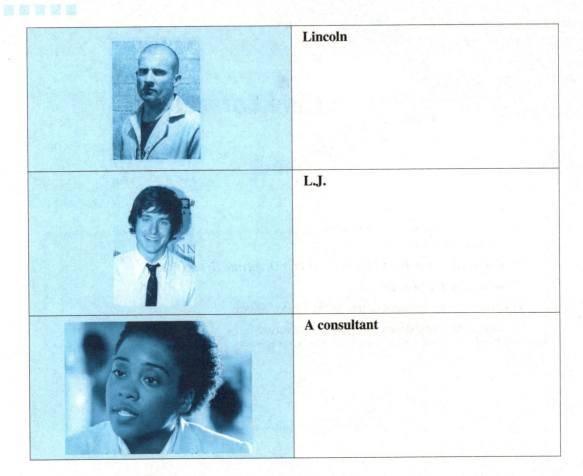

Section B　Story Retelling

Watch video clip 1 again, work in pairs and retell the story with the help of the questions and key words.

1. What are the boys doing illegally? *Key words*: pot/marijuana	2. What are the consequences of L.J.'s action according to the mother? *Key words*: set a record go to jail
3. Why are the mother and L.J. coming to visit the father in prison? *Key words*: fatherly advice	4. What are the requirements given by the lady as a consultant? *Key words*: check in scared Straight Program at Fox River mentor

Unit 10 Crime Correction

Video 2

Section A Character Introduction

Background: *Paul Young unveils his plan to build a halfway house or a community correctional center for released convicts on Wisteria Lane. Lynette learns that Paul is officially opening the halfway house and is receiving an award from the mayor for doing so. She gathers the neighborhood to start a protest during the mayor's award speech leading to a riot, which is exactly what Paul Young wanted to happen.*

Watch video clip 2 from *Desperate Housewives*, and figure out each character's attitude towards the setting up of the Community Correctional Center with your partner.

For: _____
Against: _____

美剧与美国社会文化

Section B   Story Retelling

Watch video clip 2 again, put the scenes below with key words and expressions in the right order and then retell the story.

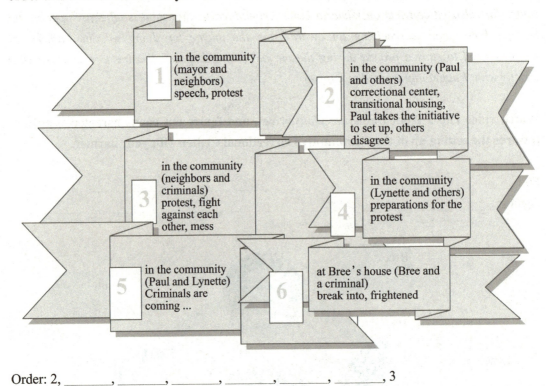

Order: 2, _____, _____, _____, _____, _____, _____, 3

Section A   Language Input

Task 1   Translate the following sentences into English, pay special attention to the parts in color, and then watch the video clip and check.

1. 你想干什么？留下案底吗？

    _____?

2. 你会坐牢的。

    _____.

3. 我们没有共同点。

    _____.

4. 上学期你还全是"优"。

    _____.

Unit 10 Crime Correction

5. 我和你对未来都充满了 希望。
   _____.

6. 你是个有潜力的孩子,你不能就这么 自毁前程。
   _____.

Task 2 Watch the video clip twice and fill in the missing information.

Lynette: "Correctional center"? What is that, a jail?
Mccluskey: I called the city. They say it's "transitional housing" for felons under _____ _____.
Bree: A halfway house for _____, on our street?
Mccluskey: Exactly.
Lynette: I don't understand. The city bought this house?
Paul: No. I did.
Lynette: You're responsible for this?
Paul: Sure I am.
Bree: What could you possibly be thinking?
Paul: The day I was _____ _____ prison, I felt so blessed. I knew that I was coming home to the loving embrace of this beautiful neighborhood. And most _____, when they're released, don't have that kind of support. Most of them are isolated, which leads them to _____ _____ _____. Bringing them to a place like this, where they can _____ _____ folks like you, might just keep a few of them from making that unfortunate choice.
Lynette: Come on, Paul. We've got children here.
Mccluskey: And I'm not spending my _____ _____ borrowing a cup of sugar from drug dealers and rapists.
Bree: I'm _____ _____ _____, but our neighborhood can't handle something like this.
Paul: _____, I have more faith in you people than you do.
Lynette: Oh, my god.
Paul: In a way, this halfway house will be a _____ to how I feel about each and every one of you.

美剧与美国社会文化

Task 3 Watch the video clip, and translate the following Chinese expressions into English.

Chinese	English
狱中老友	
迫不及待	
业主委员会	
中转屋	
设施糟糕	
贫民区	

Section B Language Output

Watch video clips in this section, and then choose one clip to dub or role play.

Clip 1: L.J., Lisa—Lincoln（in prison）
Clip 2: Consultant—L.J. (at the consultant's)
Clip 3: Paul—Lynette, Bree (in the community)
Clip 4: Paul—Lynette (in the community)

Words and Expressions

Words

agenda	[ə'dʒendə]	n.	议事日程
property	['prɔpəti]	n.	财产
incarceration	[inˌkɑːsə'reiʃən]	n.	下狱，监禁，幽闭
realtor	['riːəltə]	n.	房地产经纪人，房屋中介
hardened	['hɑːdnd]	adj.	冷酷的；坚硬的
equity	['ekwiti]	n.	公平，公正
moneybag	['mʌnibæg]	n.	钱袋，财富
felon	['felən]	n.	重罪犯
jail	[dʒeil]	n.	监狱
convict	['kɔnvikt]	n.	囚犯，罪犯
release	[ri'liːs]	vt.	释放
blessed	['blesid]	adj.	神圣的；有福的

120

Unit 10 Crime Correction

embrace	[imˈbreis]	v.	拥抱；包含；接受
inmate	[ˈinmeit]	n.	同住者；犯人；居民
rapist	[ˈreipist]	n.	强奸者
commit	[kəˈmit]	v.	犯罪；承诺；委托
charity	[ˈtʃæriti]	n.	慈善；慈善机关（团体）
pot	[pɔt]	n.	〈俚〉大麻
potential	[pəˈtenʃəl]	n.	潜力，潜能
marijuana	[ˌmɑːriˈwɑːnə]	n.	大麻
drag	[dræg]	v.	拖，拉；迫使
prior	[ˈpraiə]	n.	前科
extenuating	[eksˈtenjueitiŋ]	adj.	使减轻的；情有可原的
mentor	[ˈmentə]	n.	指导者

Phrases and Idioms

halfway house: a place where prisoners or people with mental health problems stay after they leave prison or hospital and before they start to live on their own 美国年轻犯人服刑期将满、释放前的过渡教习所

house arrest: confinement to your own home 软禁
 — He was under house arrest until the day of his trial.

jump the gun: to do something too soon, before you have thought about it carefully 草率行事
 — They jumped the gun by building the garage before permission had been given.

skid row: a city district frequented by vagrants and alcoholics and addicts（流浪汉、酒鬼经常出没的）贫民区
 — Paul was once rich, but he drank and gambled too much, and ended his life living on skid row.

screw up: make a mess of, destroy or ruin 把事情弄糟
 — She had screwed up and had to do it all over again.

Part III Culture and Society Focus

Crime in the U.S.

Crime
Youth Crime/Juvenile Delinquency
Types of Crime
Types of Youth Crime in the USA
Major Factors Leading to Crime
Major Factors for Youth Crime
Crime & Youth Crime Prevention
Crime & Youth Crime Correction

- Why is L.J. caught in *Prison Break*? And what help does he get?
- What is the so-called "correctional center" in *Desperate Housewives*?

Crime

Crime is the break of rules or laws leading to some governing authority (via mechanisms such as legal systems) ultimately prescribing a conviction. Crimes may also result in cautions or be unenforced. Crime or crimes may be defined differently by individual human societies, in different locations (state, local, international), at different time stages.

Youth Crime/Juvenile Delinquency

Juvenile delinquency, known as juvenile offending, or youth crime, refers to young individuals' involvement in illegal actions. They should be younger than the statutory age of majority. Most legal systems prescribe specific laws or regulations for dealing with juveniles, such as juvenile detention centers or correctional centers, and courts.

A juvenile delinquent refers to a person who commits an illegal behavior that should have been charged as a crime if they were an adult. A juvenile delinquent is always under the age of 18. Taking the type and seriousness of the offense committed into consideration, it is likely that those persons under 18 would possibly be charged as adults.

Unit 10 Crime Correction

Types of Crime

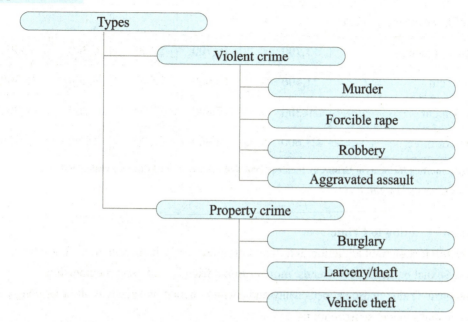

Types of Youth Crime in the USA

What can you learn from this table about Youth Crime?

School characteristic	Total number of schools	Number of schools with—			
		Violent incidents	Serious violent incidents	Theft	Other incidents
All public schools		71,000	14,300	39,300	55,900
Level:					
Primary	49200	38,500	6,400	15,000	27,100
Middle	15300	15,000	3,400	10,600	12,900
High school	11900	11,800	3,400	10,000	11,100
Combined	(NA)	(NA)	(NA)	(NA)	(NA)
Enrollment size:					
Less than 300	19,200	13,900	2,400	6,400	9,100
300 to 499	24,300	19,900	2,800	8,700	15,100
500 to 999	30,200	27,900	6,000	16,300	22,800

(continuing)

Percent of minority enrollment:					
Less than 5 percent	13,700	10,700	2,100	6,300	8,300
5 to 20 percent	21,400	17,600	2,900	9,200	13,300
20 to 50 percent	20,300	17,800	3,100	9,300	14,200
50 percent or more	27,600	24,900	6,200	14,500	20,100

Public Schools Reporting Incidents of Crime, by Incident Type and Selected School Characteristic: 2007–08
〔Source: US Census Bureau〕

Major Factors Leading to Crime

— **Adult Behavior:** alcohol addiction and illegal drug use; early involvement in first intercourse and more sexual partners; few friends, more criminal friends, and gang membership
— **Psychological Traits:** antisocial personality and attention deficit hyperactivity disorder; long-term depression and suicide; schizophrenia
— **Personality Traits:** high impulsivity, psychoticism, sensation-seeking, low self-control, high aggression in childhood, and selfishness
— **Intelligence Quotient and Learning Disabilities:** lower IQ, slow reading development and ignorance of knowledge
— **Socioeconomic Factors:** lower socioeconomic status and shorter education; high frequency of changing jobs and unemployment
— **Race, Ethnicity, and Immigration:** ethnically/racially diverse areas and immigrants related to higher crime rates
— **Religion:** high religious engagement, crucial importance of religion in one's life and membership in an organized religion

Major Factors for Youth Crime

— Poor income and living conditions adds to more risks of offending.
— Living in deteriorated inner city areas and economic and social deprivation serve as crucial predictors of committing more crimes.
— A high level of impulsiveness, hyperactivity and restlessness will be more likely to be involved in crimes.
— Low level of intelligence and poor schooling or lower academical level predict more chances of being offender.
— Poor parental supervision and harsh and critical discipline have been associated with an increased tendency of committing more crimes.
— Parental conflicts and broken families are more strongly connected with delinquency.

Unit 10 Crime Correction

Crime & Youth Crime Prevention

— *Primary prevention* lays the emphasis on individual and family level factors linked with later criminal involvement. Individual level factors such as attachment to school and engagement in pro-social activities and family level factors such as consistent parenting supervision similarly make the rate of criminal participation decline.

— *Secondary prevention* uses techniques or skills with the emphasis on at risk situations such as young persons dropping out of school or joining gangs.

— *Tertiary prevention* is adopted after a crime has occurred so that successive incidents can be stopped.

— *Situational crime prevention* uses techniques or skills with the emphasis on cutting down the opportunity to offend.

Crime & Youth Crime Correction

In criminal justice, **correction, corrections,** and **correctional,** are the special terms referring to a variety of functions typically carried out by government agencies including **imprisonment, parole** and **probation** as the punishment, treatment, and supervision of persons who have been charged of crimes. A typical correctional institution is a prison.

A correctional system with a network of agencies that administer the above functions is part of the larger criminal justice system, which additionally includes police, prosecution and courts. Jurisdictions in the US have ministries or departments, of the correctional services which are similarly named agencies.

Community Corrections

Community corrections is an integral component of the Bureau's correctional programs. Community-based correctional programs' contracts are developed and administered by community corrections staff. Through the community corrections program, the BOP (Bureau of Prisons) has developed agreements with state and local governments and contracts with privately operated facilities for the confinement of juveniles and for the detention or secure confinement of some inmates.

The BOP makes contracts with residential reentry centers (RRCs) or halfway houses, to provide assistance to inmates who are nearing release.

RRC (Residential Reentry Centers) Placement

A safe, structured, supervised environment in addition to employment counseling, job placement, financial management assistance, and other programs and services are offered by RRCs. RRCs assist inmates gradually rebuild their connections to the community and facilitate supervising ex-offenders' activities during this readjustment stage like transitional drug abuse treatment (TDAT).

— **Accountability.** RRC staff typically supervises an inmate's location and movement 24 hours a day. The contractor authorizes an inmate the right to leave the RRC with sign-out procedures for approved activities.
— **Employment.** Generally speaking, offenders are supposed to be employed 40 hours a week within 15 days after they arrive at the RRC.
— **Housing.** During their stay in RRCs, offenders have to pay a subsistence fee to help pay for their confinement, which is 25 percent of their total income, not to exceed the per diem rate for that contract.
— **Substance Abuse Treatment/Counseling.** RRCs offer drug testing and counseling for alcohol and drug-related problems.
— **Medical/Mental Health Treatment.** Usually, inmates are encouraged to take on responsibility for medical costs inhabiting in an RRC.

Home Detention

Some inmates or prisoners are required to go through home detention at the end of their prison term for the last six months or 10 percent of the sentence. Home detention is a general term referring to the fact that an inmate is required to remain at home during non-working hours of the day under some circumstances. They fulfill this part of their sentences at home within the limitations of strict schedules and curfew requirements. Sometimes electronic monitoring equipment has to be adopted to monitor those inmates.

Youth Community Corrections Bureau

This bureau offers services for helping youth reintegrating into communities. The youth offenders supervised by probation officers will receive bail orders, probation, community service orders, or other community sentences. They are provided with more opportunities to be involved in rehabilitative programs that promote positive and productive behaviors. A variety of rehabilitative services are available including mental health, specialized treatment programs, education programs and life skills training.

Youth community corrections programs include:
- Community service
- Conditional and community supervision deferred custody and supervision
- Extrajudicial sanctions program
- Fine option
- Intensive support and supervision
- Probation
- Reintegration leave

Unit 10　Crime Correction

Task 1　Warm up

What is your advice to help L.J.?

go to a Correctional Youth Center

Task 2　Preventing and Correcting Youth Crime Program

In recent years there has been an alarming rise in youth crime. Suppose you are to launch the anti-youth crime program. What are the hopeful strategies for preventing and correcting youth crime?

Step 1　Brainstorm causes or reasons attributed to youth crime.

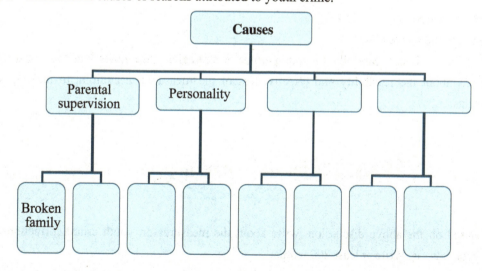

Step 2　Prepare

Make an outline.

Introduction: (Briefly state the causes.)

Body 1: (Taking the related causes into consideration, give one or two solutions on preventing youth crime and explain why some specific measures should be taken.)

Body 2: (Give one or two solutions on correcting youth crime and explain why some specific measures should be taken.)

Conclusion: (Stress the importance and urgency of the issue.)

Useful Expressions		
criminal justice	low income, poor housing	harsh and erratic discipline
commit crime	impulsiveness, hyperactivity	parental conflict
habitual offenders	low school attainment	deteriorated inner city areas

Step 3　Practice

Present it to the whole class.

Listener task: Listen carefully to your partner's strategies, take notes and then raise more questions about the feasibility and effectiveness of the measures in addition to making some comments.

Part IV　Writing

Based on the above discussion, write about the measures on youth crime corrections and give your reasons. Write at least 200 words.

Unit 10 Crime Correction

Functional Sentence Patterns

Offering Measures

Taking all these into consideration, we should ...

It is (high/about) time that something was done about it.

It is necessary that steps should be taken to ...

There is no easy method, but ... might be some help.

To solve the above mentioned problems, we must ...

Only in this way/only when ... /only through ..., can/will we ...

As long as ..., we will be able to ... /the problem is bound to ...

With the efforts of all parts concerned, the problem will be solved thoroughly.

In summary, if we continue to ignore the above-mentioned issue, more problems will crop up.

Additional Information

Prison Break	

Genre	Serial drama/Action/Crime/Thriller
Created by	Paul Scheuring
Starring	Dominic Purcell— Lincoln Burrows / Stacy Haiduk— Lisa Tabak / Marshall Allman— L.J. Burrows
Language(s)	English/ Spanish
No. of seasons /episodes	4 /81
Original channel	Fox
Original run	August 29, 2005 — May 15, 2009

Unit 11

Poverty

In this unit, you will:
- watch video clips from *Grey's Anatomy*;
- understand the lines from it;
- know something about *poverty*;
- learn some expressions on *putting forward opinions*.

Part I Story Exploration

Section A   Character Introduction

Background: Izzie Stevens is an intern in Seattle Grace Mercy West Hospital in Seattle, Washington.

Task 1 Watch the two video clips, look at the following chart of the characters, and talk about their relationship briefly.

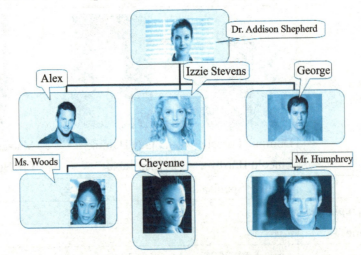

e.g. *George is Izzie's fellow intern ...*

Unit 11   Poverty

Task 2   Pair work: Use one word to describe Izzie Stevens and state your reasons.
_____ : _____

Section B   Story Retelling
Watch the two video clips again, work in pairs and retell the stories with the help of the following information.

Video clip 1:

Scene 1

Where: In Mr. Humphrey's room
Who: Izzie, Mr. Humphrey

☆ What is Izzie doing in Mr. Humphrey's room? And how does Mr. Humphrey respond?

(check, lingerie model)

_____

☆ Why does he respond in this way?

Scene 2

Where: In the locker room
Who: Alex, Izzie, George and other people
☆ What is Alex doing?

(post, tuition, bank loan)

_____

☆ How does Izzie respond?

_____

Video clip 2:

Scenes 1 & 2

Where: In Cheyenne's room
Who: Dr. Addison Shepherd, Dr. Derek Shepherd, Izzie, Cheyenne, Ms. Woods
☆ Why is Cheyenne in the hospital? Is she ready for the change in her life?

_____

☆ What do you know about Ms. Woods?

Scene 3

Where: In Cheyenne's room
Who: Izzie, Cheyenne

(give birth to, adopt, diner)

☆ What do you know about Izzie? Why does she tell her story to Cheyenne?

_____

美剧与美国社会文化

Scene 4

Where: In the lobby

Who: Izzie, Ms. Woods

☆ What makes Ms. Woods so unhappy?

_____

Scenes 5 & 6

Where: In babies' room

Who: Izzie, Cheyenne

☆ What is Cheyenne's decision?

_____

Section A Language Input

Task 1 Watch the video clip twice and fill in the missing words.

Derek:	Cheyenne, the prognosis is very good, so what we want to try to do is go in and get much the _____ out as possible during your _____.
Cheyenne:	So my baby will be fine?
Derek:	Yes.
Addison:	You may be able to take your baby home _____ _____ _____ _____ _____.
Cheyenne:	_____ _____?
Addison:	Absolutely. She'll be all yours.
Cheyenne:	Oh. Ok.
Derek:	Ok. Now, if you and your mother have any questions Dr. Stevens will _____. All right?
Addison:	See you later.
Izzie:	Oh, Shakespeare.
Cheyenne:	I was _____ _____ _____ my baby. It's really homework for English. Was. The baby wasn't _____ _____ another few more weeks. And now I guess ...
Izzie:	No more school.
Cheyenne:	It's weird. It's like when you're in school ... you hate it.
Izzie:	Until _____ _____ _____ _____.
Izzie:	Have you made any plans?

Unit 11 Poverty

Cheyenne: Plans?
Izzie: Bought a crib? Called about child care? ___ ___ ___?
Cheyenne: Not yet.
Izzie: You gonna live with your mom?
Cheyenne: I ___ ___ ___ ___ saving money to get my own trailer home. I don't know. I guess I just thought that I'd have more time. Nine months ___ ___.
Izzie: Yeah, yeah it does. I'll see you later.
Cheyenne: Bye.

Task 2 Watch the video clip twice and fill in the missing sentences.

Izzie: You're awake.
Cheyenne: Hey, yeah. Baby jumps up and down on my belly all night. ___.
… …
Cheyenne: I thought you were her mom.
Izzie: ___. … Look um I know that where we come from this kind of thing doesn't get talked about but I wanted you to know that there's more than one way to be a good mother. I wanted, ___.
Cheyenne: I love my baby.
Izzie: Of course you do. But you're reading her Shakespeare. ___, you won't be coming home and read her Shakespeare.

Task 3 Translate the following lines into English, pay special attention to the parts in color, and then watch the video clip and check.

1. 我没告诉她。我没给她建议。我也没给她压力。我只是……跟她聊了聊。
___.

2. 你有优越感。你以为你是了不起的大医生你就可以对我们的生活指手画脚?你就告诉我的孩子怎么安排她的生活?
___
___?

Section B Language Output

Watch video clips in this section, and then choose one clip to dub or role play.
Clip 1: Cheyenne—Izzie
Clip 2: Izzie—Ms. Woods

Words and Expressions

Words

biopsy	[baiˈɔpsi]	n.	活组织检查
airbrush	[ˈɛəbrʌʃ]	vt.	用喷枪去除
tattoo	[tæˈtuː]	n.	刺青
haul	[hɔːl]	vt.	拖,拉
anatomy	[əˈnætəmi]	n.	解剖
glutes	[gluːts]	n.	臀大肌的简称(gluteus)
booby	[ˈbuːbi]	n. (sl.)	女性乳房
grand	[grænd]	n. (sl.)	一千美元/英镑
amniotic fluid	[ˌæmniˈəutik ˈfluːid]		羊水
mass	[mæs]	n.	(聚成一体的)团,块,堆
obstruct	[əbˈstrʌkt]	vt.	阻塞,妨碍
airway	[ˈɛəwei]	n.	(肺的)气道
spine	[spain]	n.	脊椎,脊柱
umbilical cord	[ʌmˈbilikəl kɔːd]	n.	脐带
tumor	[ˈtjuːmə]	n.	肿瘤
charity	[ˈtʃæriti]	n.	慈善团体
surgery	[ˈsəːdʒəri]	n.	外科手术
weird	[wiəd]	adj.	奇怪的
crib	[krib]	n.	(有栏杆的)婴儿床
belly	[ˈbeli]		肚子,腹腔
figurine	[ˌfiɡjəˈriːn]	n.	小塑像,小雕像
diner	[ˈdainə]	n.	小饭店
lingerie	[ˈlɑnʒəri; læŋʒəˈriː]	n.	女性贴身内衣

Phrases

put ... through... 完成,使经历
— The trainees were put through an assault course.
build up 积累;堵塞
get a write off 勾销,注销,销账
trailer park 〈美〉活动住屋或(家庭拖车的)停车场

stuffed animal 毛绒玩具，填充玩具
big shot: *n. (informal)* an important or influential person 大人物

Bethany Whisper: 虚构的内衣公司名字，其产品专为妓女设计
Cheyenne [ʃaiˈen] 夏恩（人名）
Shepherd [ˈʃepəd] 谢泼德（姓氏）

Part III Culture and Society Focus

Section A To Be a Doctor in USA
1. American medical school tuition

Doctors are among the highest paid people in the United States, but medical school can also be a very expensive endeavor. Medical school tuition will cost at least $40,000 per year [private] or $20,000/$40,000 per year [public]. One could of course apply for a scholarship, but the competition there is pretty fierce. Most students need loans to pay for medical school and many of them finish their education heavily in debt.

According to the American Medical Association, the average debt facing graduating medical students in 2009 was $156,000.

For many students whose parents cannot afford to pay the full tuition of even the cheapest of medical schools, their dreams are all too often put on hold.

2. Terms explanation

Internship: The first year of training following medical school, also known as the first year of residency. In this period, one is called an intern (doctor).

Residency: Medical training in a specialty over a period of three or seven years. In this period, one is called a resident (doctor).

Section B

- Why did Izzie work as a lingerie model?
- When did Izzie give birth to her baby? Why did she give it up? Can you imagine her life if she kept her child?

Poverty

- What is poverty?
- Poverty Population in the USA
- Factors Leading to Poverty
- Effects of Poverty
- Poverty Reduction

What is poverty?

Poverty is defined as the state of one who lacks a usual or socially acceptable amount of money or material possessions.

Poverty is usually measured as either absolute or relative poverty.

Absolute poverty refers to the one who lacks basic human needs, which commonly includes clean and fresh water, nutrition, health care, education, clothing and shelter. About 1.7 billion people are estimated to live in absolute poverty today.

Relative poverty refers to lacking a usual or socially acceptable level of resources or income as compared with others within a society or country, and it does not imply that the person is lacking anything.

Poverty Population in the USA

According to the U.S. Census Bureau data released on September 13th, 2011, the nation's poverty rate rose to 15.1% (46.2 million) in 2010.

The government's definition of poverty is based on total income received. For example, the poverty level for 2011 was set at $22,350 (total yearly income) for a family of four.

Table 1 2012 Annual Federal Poverty Guidelines

Household size	48 Contiguous States and DC	Alaska	Hawaii
1	$11,170	$13,970	$12,860
2	15,130	18,920	17,410
3	19,090	23,870	21,960
4	23,050	28,820	26,510
For each additional person, add	$3,960	$4,950	$4,550

〔Source: Calculations by *Families USA* based on data from the U.S. Department of Health and Human Services〕

Unit 11 Poverty

Factors Leading to Poverty

Look at the following tables, what do you think lead people into poverty in USA? Are there any other factors you can think of? Discuss and share with your classmates.

Table 2

Percentage of people living in poverty	Race/ethnic group
9.9%	non-Hispanic white persons
12.1%	Asian persons
26.6%	Hispanic persons (of any race)
27.4%	black persons

〔Source: U.S. Census Bureau, 2010〕

Table 3

gender	Percentage of earning poverty level hourly wage
men	19.5%
women	31.1%

〔Source: Economic Policy Institute, 2000〕

Chart 1   In the United States, Marriage Drops the Probability of Child Poverty by 82 Percent

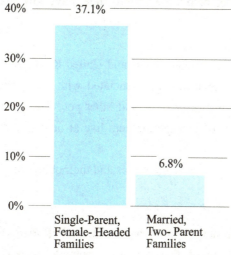

〔Source: U.S. Census Bureau, American community survey, 2007—2009 data〕

Effects of Poverty

Look at the following table, what effect of poverty is reflected here?

Table 4　In October 1996

Family income status	Percentage of 16—24 year old high school completers enrolled in college
Lower income families	48.6 %
middle income families	62.7 %
higher income families	78 %

〔Source: U.S. Department of Commerce, Bureau of the Census, Current Population Survey〕

A Trailer Park

A trailer park is a semi-permanent or permanent area for mobile homes or travel trailers. Trailer parks, especially in American culture, are stereotypically viewed as lower income housing whose occupants live at or below the poverty line, have low social status and lead a desultory and deleterious lifestyle.

Teen Pregnancy

Among developed countries, the United States and United Kingdom have the highest level of teenage pregnancy. Teenage pregnancies are associated with many social issues, including lower educational levels, higher rates of poverty, and other poorer life outcomes in children of teenage mothers. About two-thirds of teenage mothers live at or below the poverty line at the time they give birth.

Pregnancy hurts the life chances of teenage moms and their children.

Poverty Reduction

There have been many governmental and nongovernmental efforts to reduce poverty and its effects. Efforts to alleviate poverty use a disparate set of methods, such as advocacy, education, social work, legislation, direct service or charity, and community organizing.

Unit 11 Poverty

Task 1 Warm up

1. What do you think are the possible factors related to poverty? Discuss with your neighbors and fill in the following chart with the most important 4 factors respectively.

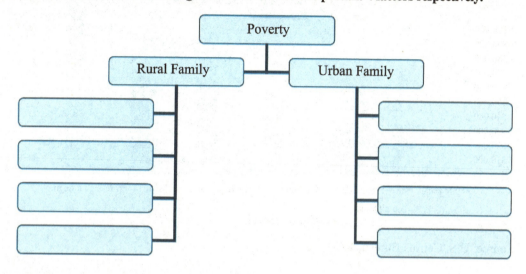

2. Work with 3 other classmates, think about ways to reduce poverty, and then report to the whole class. You can think from 2 aspects: government and individual.

Task 2 Debate: Can higher education help one get free from poverty?
In China:

A survey done by Horizon Key Research Company (零点调查公司) in 2006 showed that "education is No.1 factor causing poverty in China." When being asked about the reason causing poverty, almost a half of the poverty families mentioned "We have a college student to support." The total yearly income of 40% of the families in which there is a college student couldn't cover the student's yearly education expenses. This has affected the family's living standard severely. As a matter of fact, it is very likely that things won't turn better after the student's graduation. As s/he will face a series of financial problems, such as low pay for newly graduates, getting married, housing, etc. Thus, some parents and children choose to give up higher education.

美剧与美国社会文化

Data from USA:

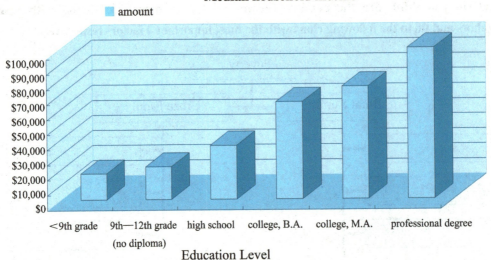

[Source: U.S. Census Bureau, 1999]

Step 1 Prepare

In this debate, your group will debate against another group.

First, discuss with your group members and the other group to decide which side you are in, to be for / against the statement that "Higher education can help one get free from poverty."

Then, work with your group members to discuss about the arguments to support your side and arguments to attack the other side. Meanwhile, the main debater should prepare a 1-minute speech about your side's opinion and main arguments.

Take notes of your arguments here:

Step 2 Debate

Debate starts with the speech of the two main debaters, and then debaters of two sides attack and defend in turn. Two students from each group work as summarizers, take notes of the debate.

Take notes of the other side's arguments and each attacking question here:

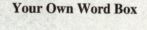

Unit 11 Poverty

Step 3 Present

The summarizers of each debate group report about the debate to the whole class.

Listener task: Take notes of the main arguments, which might be useful as material in your writing.

Useful Expressions	Your Own Word Box
wider opportunities higher standard of living higher average annual income ability to receive more promotions and raises networking and meeting new people developing communication and reasoning skills healthier outlook on life long-range outlook sacrifice current consumption opportunities go into debt	

Part IV Writing

Write about the following topic: Does Education Pay?

Based on the above debate, discuss both the two views and give your own opinion.

Give reasons for your answer and include any relevant examples from your knowledge or experience. Write at least 200 words.

> **Functional Sentence Patterns**
>
> *Putting Forward Opinions*:
> - Despite of ..., I still hold a firm belief that ...
> - Taking the above-mentioned factors into consideration, we/I may reasonably conclude that ...
> - Weighing up these arguments, I am for ...
> - It is true that ..., but one vital point is being left out, ...
> - The main problem with this argument is that it is ignorant of the basic fact that ...

Additional Information

Katherine Heigl (Izzie Stevens)

Birth Date: 11/24/1978		
Birthplace: Washington, D.C.		
Awards		
Awards (3)	TV Appearances (4)	Movies (10)
2007 Emmy Award: Outstanding Supporting Actress in a Drama Series	*Grey's Anatomy*	01/18/2008: *27 Dresses*
2007 Screen Actors Guild Award: Outstanding Performance by an Ensemble in a Drama Series	*Private Practice*	06/01/2007: *Knocked Up*
2007 People's Choice Award: Favorite Female Television Star	*The Twilight Zone*	03/16/2007: *Caffeine*
	Roswell	09/09/2005: *Side Effects* ...

Unit 12

Education and Inequality

In this unit, you will:
- watch video clips from *Gossip Girl*;
- understand the lines from it;
- know something about *education and inequality*;
- learn some expressions on *concluding*.

Part I Story Exploration

Section A Character Introduction

Background: *The students in the video clip are studying in a private school on Manhattan's Upper East Side in New York City. It is the Ivy Week for the junior class. There will be a mixer for it. The boys square up for the ushers of the mixer because they will meet the representatives from the Ivy League Schools.*

Task 1 Watch the video clip, and then put the pictures' number into correct places of the following chart.

Picture 1	Picture 2	Picture 3	Picture 4

143

美剧与美国社会文化

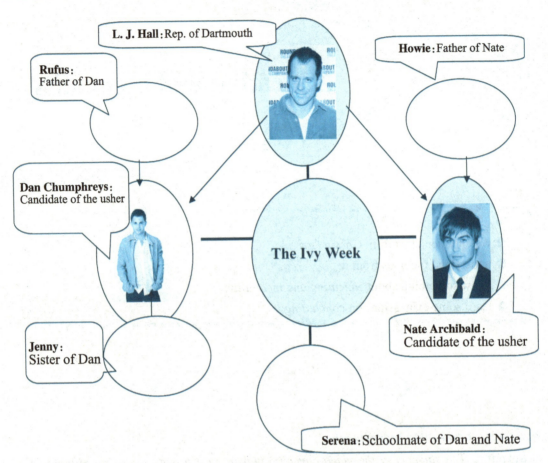

Task 2 Pair work: Use no more than three words to describe how students feel before the Ivy Week's coming.

Section B Story Retelling

Watch the video clip again, work in pairs and retell the stories with the help of the following questions.

1	What is the attitude of Dan, Dan's father, Nate and Nate's father towards the Ivy Week respectively?
2	How do Dan and Nate perform in the interview for the usher position of the mixer?
3	From Dan's perspective, why does he fail to get the post?
4	In the mixer, how is Nate's talk with L. J. Hall, rep. of Dartmouth? And then what does Dan do?

Unit 12　Education and Inequality

Part II　Language Apprecition

Section A　Language Input

Task 1　Watch the two video clips twice and fill in the missing information.

Clip 1

Voiceover: There's plenty of upside to being the spawn of the fabulously wealthy. But the downside? _____ _____ parents expect nothing less from their offspring. And when it comes to college that means the Ivies. It's more than just getting into college. It's setting a course for the _____ of _____ _____. And for those few who aren't legacies, the pressures are no less. When parents have _____ their children's futures, what kid would wanna let them down?

Clip 2

Man: And why should you be the Dartmouth usher?

Dan: Well I've given this a lot of thought and I think I can answer your question in three parts. And I'd like to start with the third part first if it's cool unless that would be confusing. In which case, I can start at the beginning. The Dartmouth "principles of community" highlight _____, _____ and _____. Well, from St. Jude's, I've learned integrity. From being an _____ _____, I have learned responsibility and from my parents, who have sacrificed everything to send me to this school, I've learned consideration. It really _____ _____ to one thing: Dartmouth is my dream and I've never asked Dartmouth but...I think it's been dreaming of me. That—that was a joke or an attempt at one.

Man: Next question...

Man: You are the _____ Dartmouth candidate.

Task 2　Read the conversation and then watch the video clip. Translate the underlined sentences to Chinese and pay special attention to the parts in color.

Howie: Try not to cut me off next time. You almost knocked me over the side of the bench.

Nate: I didn't cut you off. I didn't mean to.

Howie: (1) <u>You win fair and square and nothing could make me prouder</u>...till you get in the old Alma Mater, that is.

Nate: Dad we talked about this. (2) <u>About me keeping my options open, looking out west.</u>

Howie: Yeah, of course. But let's get serious here. Someone with your grades wants to get into Dartmouth. You need to appear to be working for it.

美剧与美国社会文化

Nate: Dad I...
Howie: Ushering the rep. is a good step.
Nate: (3) <u>How come</u> every time I <u>brought up going</u> to USC you act like it's a joke? USC — University of Southern California.
Howie: Nate, there's a plan here.
Nate: Maybe I want to make my own plan.
Howie: (4) Listen, your mother and I didn't work hard so you can just <u>make things up as you go along</u>. Dartmouth, Law school, Blair. Soon you're gonna have everything. Listen, I'm late for work. (5) <u>Nail</u> that interview today. Go, <u>green</u>!

(1) _____
(2) _____
(3) _____
(4) _____
(5) _____

Task 3 Translate the following lines into English, pay special attention to the parts in color, and then watch the video clip and check.

1. 发发小脾气，我正努力调整呢。
_____.

2. 我随时告诉你最新消息。
_____.

3. 如果你没有背景，你就是这个命了。
_____.

Section B Language Output
Watch video clips in this section, and then choose one clip to dub or role play.
Clip 1: Nate—Howie
Clip 2: Nate—Dan—Serena

Words

spawn	[spɔːn]	n.	卵,产物;(本课)孩子
fabulously	[ˈfæbjuləsli]	adv.	难以置信地,惊人地

Unit 12 Education and Inequality

offspring	[ˈɔfspriŋ]	n.	子孙,后代,孩子
legacy	[ˈlegəsi]	n.	遗产
sacrifice	[ˈsækrifais]	v.	牺牲
mixer	[ˈmiksə]	n.	交流舞会
usher	[ˈʌʃə]	n.	接待员,引座员
chipper	[ˈtʃipə]	n.	削片机;凿子
chain saw			[林]链锯,锯
hemophiliac	[ˌhiːməˈfiliæk]	n.	血友病患者
prerequisite	[ˈpriːˈrekwizit]	n.	先决条件
well-rounded	[ˈwelˈraundid]	adj.	多才多艺的,发展全面的
portfolio	[pɔːtˈfəuljəu]	n.	证券投资组合
phase	[ˈfeis]	v.	使定向,使同步
underclass	[ˈʌndəklɑːs]	n.	低年级同学;下层阶级
rehearsal	[riˈhəːsəl]	n.	预演,练习
Alma Mater (from Latin)			母校
rep	[rep]	abbr.	代表(representative)
nail	[neil]	v.	(slang)搞定
green	[griːn]	adj.	精力充沛的,意气风发的
integrity	[inˈtegrəti]	n.	正直,诚实
candidate	[ˈkændideit]	n.	候选人
endow	[inˈdau]	n.	捐赠
ironic	[aiˈrɔnik]	adj.	讽刺的
twist	[twist]	n.	扭转
hype	[haip]	n.	(本课)豪华
Bolognese	[ˌbəuləˈniːz]	n.	意大利面上的肉酱
melodramatic	[ˌmelədrəˈmætik]	adj.	夸张的,戏剧性的
stew	[stjuː]	v.	(slang)焦虑,着急
epilogue	[ˈepilɔg]	n.	结尾,收场
cop-out	[ˈkɔpaut]	n.	(slang)逃避者;虎头蛇尾
unmanned	[ˌʌnˈmænd]	adj.	无人管理的

Phrases and Idioms

let somebody down: to disappoint someone; to fail someone 让某人失望
— I'm sorry I let you down. Something came up, and I couldn't meet you.

fall back on: to depend on something after a loss or failure 依靠
— I fell back on skills I had learned years ago when I had to earn a living for myself.

美剧与美国社会文化

cut someone off: to block someone 挡路
— They cut the cattle off from the wheat field.

knock someone over: to push or strike someone or something, causing the person or the thing to fall 撞倒某人

fair and square: completely fair(ly); justly; within the rules 公正的

keep (or leave) one's options open: to wait before making a choice 再想一想
— I want to keep my options open, so I didn't sign the contract.

go along: to continue; to progress 进行,继续

make sense: to be understandable/reasonable 合情合理的

short fuse: (AmE. *slang*) a quick temper (美)急性子,火爆脾气

keep someone posted: (*fig.*) to keep someone informed (of what is happening) 随时告知某人近况
— If the price of corn goes up, I need to know. Please keep me posted.

Proper Names

The Ivies(the Ivy League Schools) 常春藤名校
the Constance Billard School 纽约贵族私立女校(虚构)
St. Jude's School 纽约贵族私立男校(虚构)
Archibald 姓氏,美国一名门望族
Dartmouth 达特茅斯学院
USC 南加州大学(University of Southern California)
Warner Bros 华纳兄弟电影公司
Faulkner 福克纳(美国小说家,曾获1949年诺贝尔文学奖)

Part III Culture and Society Focus

Section A The Ivy League

The Ivy League is an athletic conference comprising eight private institutions of higher education in the Northeastern United States. The conference name is also commonly used to refer to those eight schools as a group. The eight institutions are Brown University, Columbia University, Cornell University, Dartmouth College, Harvard University, Princeton University, the University of Pennsylvania, and Yale University. The term became official after the formation of the NCAA Division I athletic conference in 1954. The use of the phrase is no longer limited to athletics, and now represents an educational philosophy inherent to the nation's oldest

Unit 12   Education and Inequality

schools. Ivy League schools are often viewed by the public as some of the most prestigious and are often ranked among the best universities in the United States and worldwide.

Location of Ivy League Schools

Section B   Inequalities in Educational System

- For Dan, what does he depend on to get the usher position?
- Why could Nate succeed in getting the usher position?

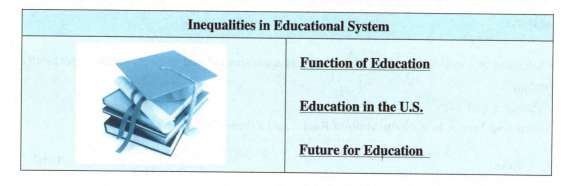

Function of Education

There are different opinions on the function of education: one is from the functional view and the other is from Conflict Theory.

The former one (T. Parsons in his *Family Socialization and Interaction Process*) argues that the function of education is to enable children to move from the particularistic standards of the family to the universal standards needed in modern adult's society. And also, students not only study from their teachers and textbooks, but their peers as well. The society and schools operate on a meritocratic basis: students achieve their status according to their merit, instead of their sex, race, or class.

But for Conflict Theory, it is believed that schools reproduce inequalities through the current educational system. The inequalities in education can all be seen concerned with "social reproduction" and "hidden curriculum."

Social Reproduction

It refers to the condition which works to maintain the cohesion of classes over time, from one generation to the next. That is to say, the members of some class use their own sources, whatever economic, political, or cultural to sustain their class identity and position.

For example, the son of an upper class lives the same way as his father: he is also a leading banker or something and lives in a luxurious villa.

Hidden Curriculum

A hidden curriculum is a side effect of an education, [lessons] which are learned but not openly intended such as the transmission of norms, values, and beliefs conveyed in the classroom and the social environment.

Although the hidden curriculum conveys a great deal of knowledge to its students, the inequality promoted through its disparities among classes and social statuses often invoke a negative connotation.

For example, students are required to be seating themselves where they are supposed to be. That is to train students with obedience and docility which may bring up non-creative generation. Another example is that due to distribution of educational resources, students in different regions are educated under different circumstances that give rise to disparity of education.

Education in the U.S.: Is there educational inequalities related to race, gender and family income?

Education and Race

Status and Trends in the Education of Racial and Ethnic Groups

Race	Associates Degree	Bachelor's Degree	Master's Degree	First Professional Degree	Total
Whites	9.3%	21.1%	8.4%	3.1%	41.9%
Blacks	8.9%	13.6%	4.9%	1.3%	28.7%
Hispanics	6.1%	9.4%	2.9%	1.0%	19.4%
Asians	6.9%	31.6%	14.0%	6.4%	46.3%
American Indians/ Alaska Natives	8.4%	9.8%	3.6%	1.4%	23.2%

〔Source: United States Department of Education — 2008〕

Unit 12   Education and Inequality

Education and Gender
The U.S. High School Completion or Higher Educational Attainment by Sex, 2000—2010

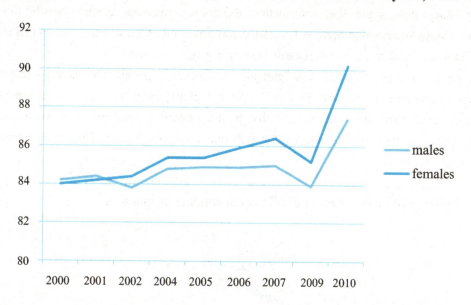

〔Source: http://www.infoplease.com/ipa/A0779809.html〕
Note: Data for 2003 and 2008 are not available.

Education and Family Income
Percentage Distribution of Credential-seeking Undergraduates, by Family Income, 2007—2008

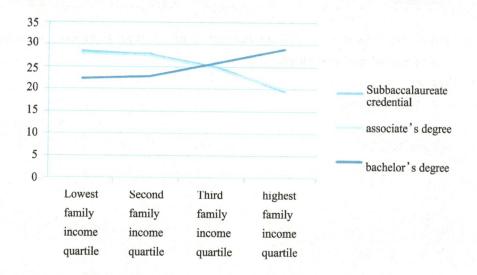

〔Source: U.S. Department of Education, National Center for Education Statistics, http://nces.ed.gov/surveys/ctes/tables/P47.asp〕

Future for Education

People have different opinions on the future of education with information technology booming. Supporters argue that information technology provides greater possibilities in education than before because there is less space and time limit. Classes and lectures can reach new students anywhere in the world, regardless of age, gender and class.

But some fear the emergence of a "computer underclass" (people who have no access to computers and do not know how to use it). As the global economy becomes increasingly knowledge- based, there is a real danger that poorer countries becomes more marginalized because of the gap between the information rich and information poor. Therefore, education inequality may reinforce.

Task 1 Brainstorm ways to ease or eradicate educational inequalities.

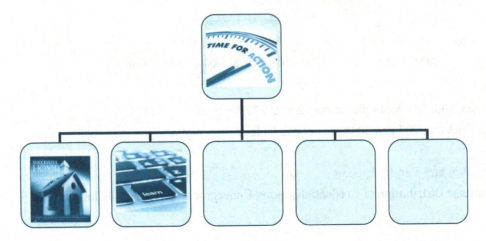

Task 2 Future for Education: Is the application of information technology an effective way to ease educational inequalities?

Step 1 Prepare

Make a list of "Yes" and "No."

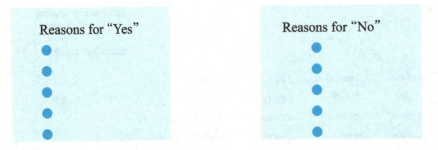

Unit 12 Education and Inequality

Step 2 Give your supporting points for your side.

Choose your side and give your supporting points (experiences, examples or any evidence).

Step 3 Rehearse and Present

First rehearse it to your partner and then present it to the whole class.

Listener task: Take notes of the main arguments, which might be useful as material for your writing.

Useful Expressions	Your Own Word Box
dissatisfaction with the educational system be unhappy about the class size teacher shortages/less funding/classroom violence escape from the confines of the classroom pick and choose what to study and when to study learn at their own pace have no access to the Internet literacy illiterate	

Part IV Writing

Write about the following topic: Online Education and De-schooling

With online education boosting, with some people's dissatisfaction with traditional schools, some people argue that there is no need for schools' existing because people can be educated online.

What is your opinion on it? Write an essay of at least 200 words on the suggested title "Online Education and De-schooling."

Functional Sentence Patterns

Concluding
- From what has been discussed above, we can draw the conclusion that...
- Therefore it is safe to draw the conclusion that...
- All reliable evidences point to one saying, that is ...

Additional Information

Gossip Girl is an American teen drama television series based on the book series of the same name written by Cecily von Ziegesar. The series was premiered on September 19, 2007. Narrated by the omniscient blogger "Gossip Girl," voiced by Kristen Bell.

Plot: The series revolves around the lives of privileged young adults on Manhattan's Upper East Side in New York City. It begins with the return of Upper East Side "It" girl, Serena van der Woodsen from a mysterious stay at a boarding school in Cornwall, Connecticut. Blair Waldorf, whom creators describe as the queen at the center of their chess game, is a longtime friend and occasional rival of Serena's, and the Queen Bee of Constance Billard School's social scene. The story also follows Chuck Bass, the bad boy of the Upper East Side; "Golden boy" Nate Archibald, Chuck's best friend and Blair's ex; and other characters of the turbulent Manhattan scene: Dan Humphrey, Nate's best friend and Serena's on-again, off-again ex; Vanessa Abrams, Dan's best friend; and Dan's sister, Jenny Humphrey.

Cultural influence: In 2008, *The New York Times* reported the show has had a profound impact on retail, saying *Gossip Girl* is probably "the first [show] to have been conceived, in part, as a fashion marketing vehicle." While it has had middling success in terms of ratings, it "may well be the biggest influence in the youth culture market," said a trend spotter.

On January 26, 2012, in honor of the series' 100th episode, New York City Mayor Michael Bloomberg visited the set and proclaimed the date Gossip Girl Day, citing the show's cultural influence and impact on the economy of the city. "*Gossip Girl* has made New York a central character. While *Gossip Girl* is drawing fans in with its plot twists, the show also attracts many of them to visit New York, contributing to our incredible 50.5 million visitors last year," he stated.

Appendix I

Useful Expressions in a Discussion/Debate

Giving personal opinion:
In my opinion, ...
From my point of view, ...
As far as I am concerned, ...
I personally think/ feel that ...

Agreeing:
I partly agree with you.
I (certainly/totally) agree with you about ...
I am (all) for it./ I have no objection.
It sounds a good idea./ That's a good point./ That's right/ correct.
Exactly./Absolutely./You bet.
I think /believe / suppose so.
I cannot agree with you more.
I feel much the same way! For example...
That's just/exactly what I was going to say!

Disagreeing:
That's quite true, but ...
Frankly, I don't like saying this, but ...
Yes, but isn't it also true that ...
I'm afraid that I can't agree with you ...
I don't agree that .../ I don't think that's right.
I see your point/ understand what you mean, but you are incorrect.

Appendix I

To be frank, I don't like your idea at all.
I'm totally against ...
It's absolutely impossible. I really can't accept the idea.

Inquiring:
What's your opinion?
What do you think of ...?
What do you suggest?/ Do you have any suggestions?

Starting a discussion:
Let's start the topic about ...
First of all, ...

Concluding a discussion:
Does anyone have anything to add up?
I'd like to sum up our discussion about ....

Appendix II

An Emmy Award is an annual television production award which is considered the television equivalent to the Academy Awards (for film), the Tony Award (for theatre), and the Grammy Awards (for music).

The two ceremonies that usually receive the most media coverage are the Primetime Emmys and the Daytime Emmys, primarily recognizing excellence in American primetime and daytime entertainment programming, respectively.

The following table is a list of TV dramas and comedies that won the Primetime Emmy Awards more than 4 times in the 20 years during 1992 to 2011. They are put in order of the times they won the Primetime Emmy Awards.

1992（44th Emmy Awards）—2011（63rd Emmy Awards）

Times of Winning the Primetime Emmy Awards	Drama/comedy	中文译名	Original Channel	Original Run
10	Law and Order	法律与秩序	NBC	1990—2010
8	Frasier	欢乐一家亲	NBC	1993—2004
7	E R	急诊室的故事	NBC	1994—2009
7	Seinfeld	宋飞传	NBC	1989—1998
7	The Sopranos	黑道家族	HBO	1999—2007
7	The West Wing	白宫风云	NBC	1999—2006

6	*Friends*	老友记	NBC	1994—2004
	The Larry Sanders Show	幕前幕后	HBO	1992—1998
	Sex and the City	欲望都市	HBO	1998—2004
	Will and Grace	威尔和格雷斯	NBC	1998—2006
	Curb Your Enthusiasm	抑制热情	HBO	2000—2005
	The Office	办公室	NBC	2005—2012
5	*NYPD Blue*	纽约重案组	ABC	1993—2005
	24	24小时	FOX	2001—2010
	30 Rock	我为喜剧狂	NBC	2006—present
4	*Mad About You*	我为卿狂	NBC	1992—1999
	The X-Files	X档案	FOX	1993—2002
	The Practice	律师本色	ABC	1997—2004
	Lost	迷失	ABC	2004—2010
	House	豪斯医生	FOX	2004—2012
	Mad Men	广告狂人	AMC	2007—present

《美剧与美国社会文化》

尊敬的老师:

您好!

为了方便您更好地使用本教材,获得最佳教学效果,我们特向使用本书作为教材的教师赠送本教材配套参考资料。如有需要,请完整填写"教师联系表"并加盖所在单位系(院)公章,免费向出版社索取。

北京大学出版社

教 师 联 系 表

教材名称	《美剧与美国社会文化》		
姓名:	性别:	职务:	职称:
E-mail:	联系电话:	邮政编码:	
供职学校:		所在院系:	(章)
学校地址:			
教学科目与年级:		班级人数:	
通信地址:			

填写完毕后,请将此表邮寄给我们,我们将为您免费寄送本教材配套资料,谢谢!

北京市海淀区成府路205号
北京大学出版社外语编辑部　郝妮娜
邮政编码:100871
电子邮箱:bdhnn2011@126.com

邮 购 部 电 话:010-62534449
市场营销部电话:010-62750672
外语编辑部电话:010-62754382